WALKING ST CUTHBERT'S WAY

MELROSE AND JEDBURGH TO HOLY ISLAND

by Rudolf Abraham

JUNIPER HOUSE, MURLEY MOSS,
OXENHOLME ROAD, KENDAL, CUMBRIA LA9 7RL
www.cicerone.co.uk

© Rudolf Abraham 2023
First edition 2023
ISBN: 978 1 78631 156 6

Printed in Turkey by Pelikan Basim using responsibly sourced paper.
A catalogue record for this book is available from the British Library.
All photographs are by the author unless otherwise stated.

For Ivana and Tamara

Updates to this Guide

While every effort is made by our authors to ensure the accuracy of guidebooks as they go to print, changes can occur during the lifetime of an edition. Any updates that we know of for this guide will be on the Cicerone website (www.cicerone.co.uk/1156/updates), so please check before planning your trip. We also advise that you check information about such things as transport, accommodation and shops locally. Even rights of way can be altered over time. We are always grateful for information about any discrepancies between a guidebook and the facts on the ground, sent by email to updates@cicerone.co.uk or by post to Cicerone, Juniper House, Murley Moss, Oxenholme Road, Kendal LA9 7RL.

Register your book: To sign up to receive free updates, special offers and GPX files where available, register your book at www.cicerone.co.uk.

Front cover: Lindisfarne Castle and harbour, Holy Island (Lindisfarne, Stage 5)

CONTENTS

Route symbols on OS map extracts

~~~ route

~~~ alternative/extension

~~~ adjacent trail

(↑) start point

(↑) finish point

(S) alternative start point

(F) alternative finish point

➤ direction of walk

Features on the overview map

——— county/unitary boundary

——— national boundary

urban area

national park

forest park/national forest
Area of Outstanding
Natural Beauty

National Scenic Area

For OS legend see OS maps.

Abbreviations

The abbreviations used for the main route names in the text are as follows:

- **SCW** St Cuthbert's Way
- **NCP** Northumberland Coast Path
- **ECP** England Coast Path
- **NST** North Sea Trail

Northumberland Coast AONB – looking southeast from the dunes at Cheswick Sands (Stage 6)

The south transept in the ruins of the 12th-century Melrose Abbey (Stage 1)

INTRODUCTION

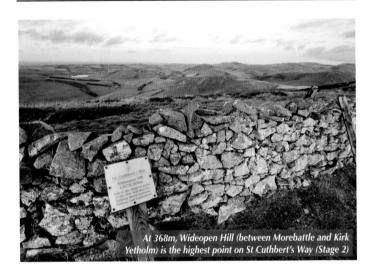

At 368m, Wideopen Hill (between Morebattle and Kirk Yetholm) is the highest point on St Cuthbert's Way (Stage 2)

For with the flow and ebb, its style
Varies from continent to isle;
Dry shod o'er sands, twice every day,
The pilgrims to the shrine find way;
Twice every day the waves efface
Of staves and sandalled feet the trace.

Marmion, Sir Walter Scott

I am inclined to think that the Cheviots are the loveliest country in England...There is an extraordinary stillness and peace in their forms; and nowhere in the world is the light and colour of sky and earth more lovely than in this bit of England.

Virginia Woolf's husband, Leonard, writing of their stay in Wooler, Northumberland, in 1914

St Cuthbert's Way is a long-distance trail that leads the walker through a series of beautiful, diverse and at times remote landscapes as it winds its way from the historic abbeys of the Scottish Borders, across the remote uplands of the Anglo-Scottish border, to the superb scenery of the Northumberland Coast.

It is a route enhanced by a wealth of birdlife, and rich with a staggering amount of historical interest. St Cuthbert's Way crosses the ancient, rugged Cheviot Hills, cloaked in pale moor-grass and studded with tors of volcanic rock, as well as the Eildon and Leaderfoot National Scenic Area; later, it passes through Northumberland National Park and the Northumberland Coast Area of Outstanding Natural Beauty. It visits some magnificent architecture, including rambling castles and medieval abbeys, as well as sites of enormous archaeological and geological interest, quiet villages, Sites of Special Scientific Interest and Special Areas of Conservation – and, come to that, some outstandingly good pubs. Access by public transport is straightforward, trails are mostly well maintained and clearly marked and the walking itself is easy.

St Cuthbert's Way stretches 62 miles (100km), from Melrose in the Borders to Holy Island, and is described in this guide as continuing up the coast to Berwick-upon-Tweed, following a stage of the Northumberland Coast Path, making a total distance of 77½ miles (125km). This allows for better transport links from Berwick, and takes in some of the most beautiful coastal scenery anywhere in Britain.

Despite its many charms, however, St Cuthbert's Way sees remarkably few walkers in comparison to most other long-distance trails in the UK. Northumberland National Park not only has the lowest population density of any national park in Britain, but also some of the lowest visitor numbers – a distinction that is both a great pity (because it is an absolutely beautiful area) and at the same time one of its great charms – it is a world away from the crowds of some of Britain's more frequented wild places.

GEOLOGY

During the Carboniferous period, around 360–290 million years ago, the area that would eventually become Northumberland and southeast Scotland was submerged beneath a shallow tropical sea, somewhere near the equator. Ages of deposition of shells and other marine life on the bed of this sea formed layers of limestone, which were then overlaid by vast amounts of mud and sediment from large river deltas. Swamps developed on these deltas and forests grew, and in time the peat and plant debris from these were covered by further layers of sedimentation. Changes in sea level caused this cycle to

View of the Northumberland coast south of the Skerrs and Cocklawburn Beach (Stage 6)

repeat itself over millions of years, creating the limestone, sandstone, coal and shale that typify the area's landscape today, and the layers of sedimentary rock so evident on the Northumberland coast, folded and faulted over subsequent millennia. Distinctive folds of limestone can be seen at Cocklawburn, between Goswick and Berwick-upon-Tweed, and limestone bands project into the sea nearby as the Skerrs. Inland, the fell sandstone formed during this period can be seen in the Simonside Hills and in the rocks that form St Cuthbert's Cave.

The single most distinctive geological feature running across this landscape is the Whin Sill. A great elongated sheet of dolerite rock, it was formed when molten rock oozed up through cracks and fissures in the earth's crust then spread out between layers of sedimentary rock, during the end of the Carboniferous period, some 295 million years ago. Its distinctive vertical cracks and columns were formed as the molten rock cooled. The Whin Sill stretches from one side of the county to the other, and upon its hard outcrops are built many of Northumberland's most prominent monuments, including Hadrian's Wall, Lindisfarne Castle and Bamburgh Castle. In the east it splinters off the Northumberland coast in features such as Harkess Rocks near Bamburgh, making its easternmost appearance with the Farne Islands, and its southernmost appearance near Craster, at Cullernose Point. Dolerite is often known as whinstone in Northumberland.

The Cheviots were formed during the Devonian period, some 380 million years ago, and are the remnants of volcanoes and their huge lava flows, which covered an area of some 230 square miles (600km²). An enormous mass of granite was later intruded beneath these volcanoes, and it is the upper levels of this granite core, exposed by eons of subsequent erosion, which now form these hills. The volcanic cones themselves have long gone. The heat from these later intrusions 'baked' and further hardened the existing lava with which it came into contact, and it is this metamorphosed rock that forms the familiar rocky tors of the Cheviots. Further north, in the Borders, the Eildons also constitute the remnants of a laccolith or volcanic intrusion.

Successive periods of glaciation from around 2 million to 12,000 years ago scoured the landscape and shaped it into its present form, leaving the broad, familiar U-shaped valleys, as well as meltwater channels (particularly clear on Humbleton Hill in the Cheviots) and the vast, undulating and mineral-rich deposits that coat much of the landscape today. These glaciers also carried and deposited rocks far from their geological origin – attested by the presence of blocks of volcanic rock from the Cheviots on the Northumberland and Yorkshire coasts.

Sand dunes form a fairly narrow band along parts of the Northumberland coast, the largest and most extensive of these being found at Cheswick Sands and Goswick Sands, and the Snook on Holy Island. While there are some very

Statue of St Cuthbert by Fenwick Lawson, in the ruins of Lindisfarne Priory, Holy Island (Stage 5)

old dunes based on glacial sands and clays in Lindisfarne National Nature Reserve (Ross Links, for example, on the mainland south of Holy Island, contains some of the oldest dunes in Britain), the majority of sand dunes on the Northumberland coast are relatively young, formed over the last 200–300 years. Due to their age, the older dunes are more acidic, which is reflected in the plant species that grow there.

WEATHER

Northumberland's geographical position on the northeast coast of England acts as a moderating influence as far as climate is concerned – meaning that although statistics point to it being on average the coldest county in England, it escapes the extremes of some other areas in the UK.

Summer temperatures on the Northumberland coast reach an average daytime high of around 18°C in July and August, with an average low of 10.8°C for the same months. June and September have average maximum temperatures of 15.6°C and 15.9°C, respectively, and average minimum temperatures of 8.6°C and 9.1°C; the same values for May and October are 12.5°C/5.9°C and 12.8°C/6.7°C, respectively. January has the lowest average temperatures, with an average maximum of 6.7°C and an average minimum of 1.3°C (although in January 1982 it plummeted to –12.3°C), with February only very marginally higher. May and June see the greatest number of hours of sunshine, followed by July and August. Average sea surface temperatures on the Northumberland coast are, as might be expected, quite low (around 13°C in summer, compared to 18°C on England's southwest coast).

Inland in the Scottish Borders, temperatures are similar to those on the coast but decrease with altitude – thus, upland areas such as the Cheviots will be several degrees cooler. Yetholm has an average maximum January temperature of 6°C, and an average January minimum of 1°C. The corresponding values for July and August in Yetholm are 20°C and 10°C. Wind chill must be added to these temperatures, which will make them feel considerably cooler.

Rainfall in the Borders and Northumberland is less than experienced in the northwest of England, with an average annual precipitation of 651mm on the coast, and between 890mm (low-lying areas) and 1145mm (The Cheviot) in Northumberland National Park. In the Borders, Yetholm has an average annual precipitation of 603mm. Compare these figures with the Lake District, which has an average annual precipitation of over 3200mm in some areas. November is usually the wettest month, with an average rainfall of 67.2mm on the Northumberland coast, while July typically sees the least rainfall of the

The author's daughter walking on Cheswick Sands (Stage 6)

summer months (47.6mm) and August the most (62.1mm). Yetholm usually experiences the heaviest rainfall in October (73mm).

Snowfall occurs mainly in January and February, but snow can fall any time between November and March in the hills, with snow lying on average 10 days a year on the coast, more in the hills.

Winds are for the most part moderate, and gusts rarely reach above 18 knots in the summer – although winds reaching gale force are not unknown, despite being uncommon. The windiest months on the coast are December to March, with average gusts reaching over 30 knots; the calmest months are June, July and August.

Nevertheless, bear in mind that all these figures are averages, and variations can be considerable – so check local weather forecasts (see www.metoffice.gov.uk and www.mwis.org.uk). As an example, in the winter of 2010 heavy snowfall began in November (around 30cm in one day, including the coast) and continued for several days, with temperatures dipping to around –9°C in Northumberland.

WILDLIFE AND PLANTS

Wildlife

The landscape of Northumberland and the Borders is home to an extraordinarily rich and diverse range of wildlife. Its forests are one of the last strongholds of Britain's native red squirrel population – more than half

Eider ducks, Holy Island Causeway (Stage 5)

the entire UK red squirrel population lives in Kielder Forest alone – while otters still live alongside its remote, clear streams and burns, stoats and weasels can be seen scampering among its hedgerows, and roe deer and feral goats wander its rugged hills. Minke whales, dolphins and grey seals can all be seen off the Northumberland coast – even a lone humpback whale has been spotted in these waters, as have basking sharks – while salmon and sea trout swim up its rivers to spawn, and some of its shallow lakes are home to Britain's only native species of freshwater crayfish.

The River Tweed is particularly well known for its salmon, while the Farne Islands are home to one of the most important colonies of grey seals in Europe, some 3000–4000 strong. There is an enormous variety of birdlife, from raptors to seabirds,

waterfowl and waders. The Farne Islands are home to four of the five species of British tern (including Arctic and roseate tern), as well as puffins and guillemots. Eider ducks are found here, too; they are sometimes known locally as 'cuddy ducks', referring to St Cuthbert who is said to have placed the birds under special protection following his sojourn on the Farnes in the seventh century. Other birds you are likely to see on the coast include curlew, Mediterranean gull, kittiwake, razorbill and redshank.

During the winter months, Northumberland becomes a temporary home to numerous species of birds migrating from further north – from Iceland, Greenland, Svalbard and Scandinavia. Some stop here only briefly before continuing their migration; others remain throughout the winter, before returning to their

Donkeys outside the village of Kirk Yetholm in the Borders (Stage 3)

breeding grounds in the frozen north. These winter migrants are to be found in particular in the enormous tidal area south of Holy Island on the Northumberland Coast AONB, Fenham Flats, which forms part of Lindisfarne National Nature Reserve, and nearby Budle Bay. They can be seen here in their thousands – from great skeins of shelduck flying overhead, to huge flocks of grey plover grazing on the tidal flats.

Fenham Flats is home during the winter to no fewer than six internationally important species of wildfowl and wading bird. The pale-bellied brent goose, which arrives from its breeding grounds in the Svalbard archipelago, and for whom this is the only regular wintering site in Britain, is joined by pink-footed and greylag geese, wigeon, grey plover and bar-tailed godwits. The whooper swan (distinguishable from the mute swan by its longer, predominantly yellow bill with a black tip) is another of the winter migrants you might see further inland, sometimes from as early as late October.

Inland, the scarce black grouse can be spotted on the Cheviots, in particular in the College Valley. Other species to look out for in the Cheviots include ring ouzel, whinchat and curlew – the latter forming the logo of Northumberland National Park. Ospreys can also be seen at Kielder Water – the first chicks born in Northumberland for over 200 years were hatched there in 2009.

Moths, including the emperor moth and northern eggar, are found on areas of heather moorland, and around half the English and Welsh population of the large heath butterfly is found in Northumberland National Park.

Plants

The extensive dune systems of the north Northumberland coast are colonised by species such as marram grass and ragwort, and in more stable areas can be found flowers, including rest harrow and bloody cranesbill – county flower of Northumberland. Specialised species such as silverweed and marsh helleborine grow in the dune slacks (hollows behind the dunes which are below the water table for at least part of the year). Among those species found among the older dunes of Lindisfarne National Nature Reserve is the recently discovered endemic Lindisfarne helleborine.

Areas of whin grassland (so called because of the hard, dense whinstone that lies beneath it) are found along the coast, with species such as lyme grass, common rock rose and maiden pick, while bell heather and sedges grow among areas of coastal heathland. Coastal cliff faces are often rich in mosses and lichens, and also support species such as red fescue and spring squill. Eelgrass grows among the mudflats, and pink thrift appears in spring in areas of saltmarsh.

Invasive species include piri piri burr from New Zealand (found on

A blaze of late autumn colour on the Cheviots (Stage 3)

Holy Island, among other places); you can help prevent this spreading further by picking the burrs off your boots and trouser legs rather than inadvertently transporting them to other areas.

Inland from the coast, the upland areas of Northumberland National Park are typified by hardy grasses such as moor-grass and mat-grass, as well as heather – although less widespread on the Cheviots than an area such as Simonside, partly as a result of overgrazing.

Several areas of blanket bog survive in Northumberland National Park, fragile and ancient ecosystems typified by cushions of sphagnum moss, which support species such as sundew and asphodel. Recently, conservation efforts have allowed several areas of bog – formerly drained

in the process of land reclamation – to become waterlogged again (by blocking drainage channels), so that plant communities can re-establish themselves.

Woodland mostly takes the form of forestry plantations, many of these planted by the Forestry Commission to provide forestry reserves following World War 2. Nevertheless, there are still a few highly prized fragments of the ancient, semi-natural woodland that would have once covered much of this landscape – among them Harrowbog in the College Valley, which lies within Northumberland National Park. Species in such areas of natural woodland include oak, ash, juniper, downy birch and wych elm.

The plantations that now dot the landscape range in size from small patches of trees to the enormous Kielder Forest, which covers an area of some 250 square miles (402km²), making it the largest forest in England. However, in the College Valley, some 55,000 deciduous trees were planted in 1995, constituting the largest new 'native' woodland in England.

There are also a number of historic gardens in the region, foremost among these being the gardens at Belsay Hall.

EILDON AND LEADERFOOT NSA

The Eildon and Leaderfoot National Scenic Area – the Scottish equivalent of an AONB – covers an area of around 14 square miles (36km²), encompassing the Eildon Hills, Melrose and the valleys of the River Tweed and Leader Water. The Tweed and its catchment area are an SSSI. St Cuthbert's Way crosses the Eildons on its first stage, immediately after leaving Melrose, before following the course of the Tweed for a short distance. The area was designated an NSA in 1980.

NORTHUMBERLAND NATIONAL PARK

Northumberland National Park was created in 1956, and covers an area of around 405 square miles (1049km²) between Hadrian's Wall in the south, Kielder Water in the west, the Cheviots and the Scottish border in the north, and Wooler and Rothbury in the east. Within this area are no fewer than 32 Sites of Special Scientific Interest (SSSIs), including the Cheviot tors, 6 Special Areas of Conservation (SACs), 3 National Nature Reserves (NNRs) and a RAMSAR site (wetlands of international importance) at Holburn Lake and Moss, as well as several sites of exceptional historical and archaeological interest.

The landscape of the national park ranges from the rugged, rolling Cheviots to outcrops of the Whin Sill along the course of Hadrian's Wall, fell sandstone and heather moorland, shallow freshwater lakes, forest and peat bogs. The highest point in the national park is The Cheviot (815m).

The northernmost national park in England and Wales, Northumberland National Park has the lowest population density of any national park in England and Wales by a significant margin (a total of only around 2000 people, compared to over 42,000 in the Lake District National Park, which covers an area slightly more than double its size). Its annual visitor numbers are equally low – 1.5 million, compared to 15.8 million in the Lake District National Park and 9.5 million in the Yorkshire Dales National Park.

St Cuthbert's Way crosses part of Northumberland National Park in the north, following a route through the Cheviots between the Anglo-Scottish border and Wooler.

Wide Open Hill (Stage 2)

NORTHUMBERLAND COAST AONB

Designated in 1958, the Northumberland Coast Area of Outstanding National Beauty covers an area of around 85 square miles (138km²), along a narrow, 39-mile (64km) strip of coastline between Berwick-upon-Tweed in the north and the Coquet estuary in the south.

It includes 12 SSSIs (among these Alnmouth saltmarsh and dunes and Bamburgh dunes), 3 Special Protected Areas (SPAs) and 2 SACs, and is a RAMSAR site, while Holy Island (Lindisfarne) and the Farne Islands are both NNRs.

St Cuthbert's Way enters the AONB near Holy Island, and a recommended extension to the route then follows the coast up to Berwick-upon-Tweed, along part of the Northumberland Coast Path (which covers the whole length of the AONB, from Cresswell to Berwick-upon-Tweed).

HISTORY AND HERITAGE

Stone Age and Iron Age

The earliest evidence of human habitation in the area dates from the Mesolithic Period (Middle Stone Age), mostly in the form of stone tools and delicately worked arrowheads, used by the hunter-gatherers who hunted in its woodlands and grasslands, and fished its coastal waters.

The Northumberland landscape is exceptionally rich in rock art, including large numbers of the enigmatic although strangely beautiful cup-and-ring markings. There are over 1000 recorded examples of this rock art in Northumberland, much of which was little known or appreciated until comparatively recently. Dating from the Neolithic Period (New Stone Age, around 4500–2000BC, a period marked by the gradual adoption of agriculture and the domestication of livestock), it is scattered widely across the area, with several examples on or close to the route of St Cuthbert's Way (for instance, Weetwood Moor, just outside Wooler, and Doddington Moor to the north of this). The meaning of these markings is unknown – although their placement (near a spring or watercourse, or in an area of upland pasture) appears to have been carefully chosen.

The largest Iron Age fort in Northumberland, Yeavering Bell, is passed on St Cuthbert's Way, between Hethpool and Wooler;

and one of the Eildon Hills, just outside Melrose at the beginning of St Cuthbert's Way, was also the site of an enormous Iron Age hill fort. Both were once occupied by the powerful Votadini tribe, an Iron Age people made up of several smaller tribes. Numerous other hill forts, cairns (burial mounds) and cists (stone-lined burial chambers) are dotted across the landscape.

Roman Britain

The preeminence of the Votadini was curtailed by the arrival of the Romans in the first century AD. Over the next 300 years the Romans introduced a period of stability in these borderlands, building a network of roads (two of which, Dere Street and the Devil's Causeway, are

Boat hulls beside Lindisfarne Castle, Holy Island (Stage 5)

ST CUTHBERT

St Cuthbert was probably born around AD634, in southern Scotland or Northumbria, and began his ministry at Melrose in about 650. He accompanied Eata, Abbot of Melrose, to establish a new monastery at Ripon in what is now North Yorkshire, then became Prior of Melrose Abbey in 664. Cuthbert travelled widely, preaching the gospels in remote villages and becoming renowned for his piety. Later, in 676, he adopted the life of a hermit, taking up residence on one of the Farne Islands. It was during this period that he is said to have placed eider ducks – which still live on the Farnes – under special protection; for this reason, they are still often called 'cuddy ducks' in Northumberland. In 684 he was elected Bishop of Hexham, but instead accepted the position of Bishop of Lindisfarne – a setting which, by its geographical location just north of the Farne Islands, was evidently much closer to his heart.

Cuthbert died on the Farnes in AD687 and was buried at Lindisfarne. In 875, following Viking raids, his remains were removed by the monks of Lindisfarne, and were later buried at Durham.

Both during his lifetime and after his death, Cuthbert was frequently associated with miracles. According to Bede, his body was found to be miraculously preserved when his coffin was opened 11 years after his death; and the ninth-century king Alfred the Great claimed to have had a vision or dream of St Cuthbert which inspired him in his resistance against the Vikings.

A small book placed in Cuthbert's tomb but removed in the 12th century, known as the St Cuthbert Gospel – the earliest intact European book, with one of the earliest surviving intact bindings – was purchased by the British Library in 2012. Dating from the early 8th century, it contains a copy of the Gospel of John, beautifully written, in Latin.

From the eighth century, Britain witnessed successive waves of devastating Viking raids, the first recorded of these taking place on Lindisfarne in 793. By 866 the Vikings had taken York, installing a puppet king in Bernicia, and in 875 the monks of Lindisfarne Priory were forced to flee Holy Island with the remains of St Cuthbert and other relics. The monks are said to have rested at St Cuthbert's Cave (on St Cuthbert's Way), and St Cuthbert's remains were later buried at Chester-le-Street, before finding their final resting place in Durham Cathedral in 995.

encountered on the routes in this guide) and, from AD122, Hadrian's Wall – a great string of earthworks, milecastles, forts and turrets that

ST OSWALD

Oswald was born around AD605, the son of Aethelfrith, King of Bernicia, and Queen Acha of Deira. Following his father's death in 616 at the hands of Edwin of Deira, the young Oswald fled to western Scotland, where he converted to Christianity under the influence of monks from the island of Iona. When Edwin was killed by Caedwalla of Gwynedd and Penda of Mercia, Oswald returned to Bernicia with a small army, confronting them at Heavenfield in 634 or 635. According to the eighth-century historian Bede, Oswald erected a large wooden cross on the eve of battle and asked his soldiers to pray for victory. Their ensuing rout of the combined Welsh and Mercian forces – which greatly outnumbered Oswald's – was subsequently attributed to this act of faith.

Oswald's claim to both crowns enabled him to reunite both Bernicia and Deira into one of the most powerful kingdoms of medieval Britain, Northumbria, its territory stretching as far north as the Firth of Forth. He invited an Irish monk, St Aidan, to found a priory on Holy Island (Lindisfarne) in 635 and help spread Christianity in Northumbria.

In 642, Oswald was killed in battle against his old enemy Penda at Oswestry ('Oswald's Tree') in Shropshire. Penda ordered Oswald's body to be hacked to pieces and his head and arms displayed on stakes, although some of his remains were later recovered by Oswald's brother Oswiu. His head was taken to Lindisfarne, but removed when the monks there fled the Viking raids of the ninth century, and eventually came to rest in St Cuthbert's Tomb at Durham Cathedral. Oswald's reign was particularly significant in terms of the more widespread introduction of Christianity in northern England.

arguably constitute the most memorable Roman archaeological remains anywhere in the UK.

The Anglo-Saxon period

During the fifth century, the Angles (a people from the borderlands between Germany and Denmark) and the Saxons (from northern Germany) invaded Britain, filling the power vacuum created by the departure of the Romans. The Angle King Ida took Bamburgh on the northeast Northumberland coast in AD547, naming his new kingdom in northeast England and southeast Scotland Bernicia. Ida's grandson Aethelfrith carved out an enormous territory, but following his death Edwin, prince of the neighbouring kingdom of Deira (between the Humber and the Tees), seized the throne, establishing a royal palace at Ad Gefrin (Old Yeavering, near Kirknewton and not far from St Cuthbert's Way). Edwin was later defeated by the Mercians, led by a chieftain named Penda, and the Welsh king Caedwalla, in AD633, with Aethelfrith's eldest son taking the throne in Bernicia – although he, too, soon met his end. His brother Oswald defeated Caedwalla and Penda at Heavenfield, near Hadrian's Wall, in around 635. Attributing his victory to the Christian faith, Oswald set about introducing Christianity to his kingdom. From his capital at Bamburgh he invited St Aidan, an Irish monk from the monastery on Iona, to Bernicia. Aidan settled with a small group of monks on the island of Lindisfarne (Holy Island), and was later followed by St Cuthbert, prior of the abbey at Melrose. Holy Island was to become one of the most important early centres of Christianity in England, and it was here that the Lindisfarne Gospels – one of the most beautiful medieval manuscripts to have survived to the present day – were created in the early years of the eighth century (search for 'The Lindisfarne Gospels' on www.bl.uk).

It is on these events of the seventh century and St Cuthbert's journey from Melrose that the route of St Cuthbert's Way is based.

The Medieval period

Uprisings in York, Durham and elsewhere following the Norman conquest led to William the Conqueror laying waste to much of the northeast – so much so that England north of the River Tees was not even included in the Domesday Book of 1086. The Scottish King David I invaded northern England in 1138, and the following year the Anglo-Scottish border was established on the River Tees – although by 1157 Northumberland had been reclaimed by England under Henry II.

From the early 12th century many of the region's great abbeys, sacked or destroyed during the Viking raids of previous centuries, were restored or rebuilt, including Lindisfarne, and new monasteries were built at Melrose.

John Balliol was installed as the Scottish king in 1292, after several years of interregnum following the death of Alexander III (who left no direct heir), under the 'arbitration' of the English King Edward I. Edward invaded Scotland in 1296, and from this date England and Scotland were plunged into a long, protracted period of conflict, with the border areas suffering frequent damage from passing armies. Berwick-upon-Tweed passed back and forth several times between English and Scottish rule during this period, and the great abbeys at Melrose and Dryburgh were both sacked in the 14th century. Perhaps not surprisingly, this period also coincided with the building or refortifying of some of the greatest castles in the area.

In 1377 Henry Percy was made the first Earl of Northumberland. The Percy family, one of the most powerful

Jedburgh Abbey portal (Stage 2)

noble families in northeast England, were descended from William de Percy, who had arrived from Normandy with William I. Perhaps the most famous Percy was the first Earl's son, also called Henry – most of the Percys were called Henry or William – better known as 'Harry Hotspur'. The Percys supported Henry VI and the House of Lancaster during the War of the Roses in the 15th century, several battles of which were fought in Northumberland, although later the fourth Earl was forced to switch his allegiance to Edward IV and the House of York.

The Tudor period
In 1513 the forces of the Scottish King James IV were defeated at Flodden Field, a few miles north of Yeavering Bell and St Cuthbert's Way, by the English army of Henry VIII. Attacks were made on the Borders in the 1530s, and in the widespread destruction of these campaigns and the 'Rough Wooing' of the 1540s (in which Henry VIII attempted to force Mary Queen of Scots to marry his son Edward), the abbeys at Melrose and Dryburgh were torched. Henry VIII's dissolution of the monasteries in 1536–1540 sounded the death knell for the other abbeys in this region, as elsewhere.

In the 16th century, Berwick-upon-Tweed's defences gained an elaborate, Italianate system of bastions and fortifications, the like of which had probably never been seen this far north in Europe at that time, and which still constitute the finest Elizabethan fortifications in Britain.

Border Reivers

The instability and frequent devastation experienced by the border regions from the late 13th century onwards – and the hardship this imposed on the area's inhabitants – led to a general state of lawlessness, and the rise of the Reivers. Raiders from both England and Scotland, the Reivers took livestock and other possessions from pretty much anyone not attached to their own families or protected by someone more powerful – a state of affairs that explains the presence of many pele towers and bastles (fortified houses) in the region. The Reivers were transported to Ireland by James I (VI of Scotland) in the early 1600s.

The 18th and 19th centuries

During the 18th and 19th centuries, an important lime industry developed in Northumberland, particularly along the coast. The lime was burnt in large brick kilns for agricultural use; initially, single or small groups of kilns supplied local farms, but from the late 18th century lime was exported by sea (and later by rail), with larger groups of kilns being built, such as those on Holy Island. Perhaps the best illustration of these kilns in action is a large painting in the entrance hall of Lindisfarne Castle, which depicts the limekilns blazing beside the castle at night. Coal was also mined locally (and used, for example, to fire the limekilns) – the lighthouse at the Snook on Holy Island is said to have been built over a mine shaft. Sandstone was quarried widely, providing stone for local buildings, from farm walls and cottages to bridges, castles and abbeys.

19th-century lime kilns near Lindisfarne Castle, Holy Island (Lindisfarne, Stage 5)

WW2 anti-tank blocks (Stage 5)

The First and Second World Wars

The global conflicts of the 20th century have also left their mark on the region. The Otterburn ranges were the site of an elaborate network of trenches, which were dug as a practice area for the trench warfare of the Western Front during World War 1. During World War 2, the low, flat, open expanses of the north Northumberland coast were one of the suspected points of a projected land invasion by Hitler's Germany – and this part of England still bears numerous reminders of this period of history.

Pillboxes in various states of preservation are encountered at several points along and just inland from the coast (there are 37 of them within the Northumberland Coast AONB alone), and large concrete anti-tank blocks still lie along some beaches as well as by the entrance to the Lindisfarne causeway. The tidal flats around Holy Island – now part of Lindisfarne National Nature Reserve – were used for live bombing practice, while the remote hilltops of the Cheviots are scattered with the wrecks of World War 2 bombers and fighter planes that smashed into their flanks during poor weather or low visibility.

TRANSPORT

The assumption that you need a car to explore the remote areas of Northumberland and the Borders is misplaced, at least for the areas covered by the route in this guide. While there certainly are places that have no public transport, the trailheads (start/finish points) of St Cuthbert's Way are easily accessible by bus or train, and the towns and villages where you are likely to start/finish the various stages of these walks are well served by local buses. Even a village such as Kirk Yetholm – hardly on the

25

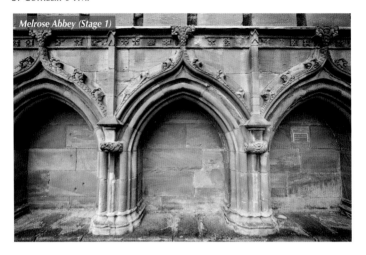

Melrose Abbey (Stage 1)

main road to anywhere – has half a dozen buses a day to Kelso, from where there are regular connections to Berwick-upon-Tweed, Edinburgh and other towns in the Borders.

In any case, since St Cuthbert's Way is a point-to-point, rather than circular, route, taking a car to the start of the walk would only mean having to return – by public transport – to pick it up after finishing the walk several days later.

The obvious, easiest and certainly the most pleasant way of getting to northeast Northumberland is by train. London North Eastern Railway (LNER, www.lner.co.uk) has fast, regular services between London Kings Cross and Edinburgh, calling at Newcastle and Berwick-upon-Tweed. Book in advance to take advantage of discounted online fares.

Those places not served by rail are easily reached by bus, even off-season. To get to Melrose (for the start of St Cuthbert's Way), there is a service from Berwick-upon-Tweed (67). In addition, there are several services running to towns and villages passed on the route. The X18 is useful for getting around the towns and villages of the north Northumberland coast, while the 477 provides an albeit infrequent service for those who wish to get direct from Holy Island to Berwick-upon-Tweed.

For convenience, the main bus services you are likely to use in connection with St Cuthbert's Way are as follows (all services daily, usually with reduced services on Sundays, unless otherwise specified):

Arriva (www.arrivabus.co.uk)
- X15 Newcastle–Berwick-upon-Tweed via A1 (Morpeth, Felton, Alnwick, Belford, Beal)
- X18 Newcastle–Berwick-upon-Tweed via coast (Morpeth, Warkworth, Alnmouth, Alnwick, Craster, Beadnell, Seahouses, Bamburgh, Belford, Beal)
- 685 Newcastle–Carlisle

Border's Buses (www.bordersbuses.co.uk)
- 51 Jedburgh–Edinburgh (also stops at Ancrum and St Boswells)
- 60 Berwick-upon-Tweed–Galashiels (also stops at Melrose)
- 61 Galashiels–Melrose (Mon–Sat)
- 67 Berwick-upon-Tweed–Melrose (also stops at St Boswells)
- 68 Jedburgh–Galashiels (also stops at Ancrum and St Boswells)
- 81 (Mon–Sat,) Kelso–Yetholm
- 267 (Mon–Sat) Berwick-upon-Tweed–Wooler (via Etal)
- 464 (Mon–Sat) Berwick-upon-Tweed–Wooler (via Lowick)
- 477 (Mon–Sat) Berwick-upon-Tweed–Holy Island (also stops at Beal/Holy Island Road end)
- X62 Edinburgh–Galashiels
- X95 Carlisle – Galashiels – Edinburgh

Glen Valley Tours (www.glenvalley.co.uk, tel 01668 281578)
- 710 (Wed and Sat) Kelso–Newcastle (via Wooler and Morpeth)

These details were correct at the time of writing; however, always check locally for possible changes either to routes or service providers.

For timetables see individual bus company websites or for services in Northumberland go to www.northumberland.gov.uk/Highways/Public-transport.aspx.

ACCOMMODATION

Accommodation on and around St Cuthbert's Way is provided by a good range of B&Bs, inns and small hotels, some of them outstanding. Some B&Bs can also provide evening meals and packed lunches by prior arrangement, otherwise there is usually a decent (or, more often, excellent) pub or inn nearby. There are a few youth hostels, although not enough to base the route on entirely.

Camping is somewhat limited: with the exception of the northern part of the coast, there are not really many campsites on the route itself and camping is prohibited in Northumberland National Park.

Prices on Holy Island are generally higher than elsewhere on the coast, and some places require a minimum three-night stay. Despite the fact that Northumberland is often described as England's 'best-kept secret', it pays to book well in advance, especially on the coast in the summer – on some stages there are only a few places providing accommodation.

Suggestions of places to stay are given in the introduction to each stage, which can in most cases be considered a personal recommendation; Appendix D lists further accommodation options.

ABOUT THE ROUTES

No technical difficulties are encountered on St Cuthbert's Way or the Northumberland Coast Path, and the walk can safely be described as easy. There are no high-level or exposed sections. Some of the stages are quite long, however, and some of the stiles can be quite steep. The crossing of Gains Law and Humbleton Hill in the northern Cheviots on St Cuthbert's Way could cause navigation problems in low cloud or poor weather, and both these areas can be exposed to strong winds.

St Cuthbert's Way covers 77½ miles (125km), including the route from Holy Island to Berwick-upon-Tweed along the Northumberland Coast Path. The highest point on St Cuthbert's Way is 368m (Wideopen Hill) and crossing the Cheviots is somewhat elevated as well. There is the possibility of making short detours to higher ground – Mid Eildon (422m), for example. Around half of St Cuthbert's Way is in the Borders, and half in Northumberland. It crosses areas of Northumberland National Park (the Cheviots).

You may encounter a few unfamiliar words and place names while walking St Cuthbert's Way, drawn from the rich local dialects in Northumberland and the Borders, some of them Anglo-Saxon in origin (see Appendix B).

WHEN TO GO

St Cuthbert's Way can be walked at any time of year. However, as noted above, the weather is generally at its finest from May to July, and as a result this period together with August sees the largest number of visitors. December and January are usually the wettest months – although sustained periods of fine weather are not impossible in January in the Borders, on the Northumberland coast and in Northumberland National Park. Winter walking over snow-covered hills can be extremely beautiful for those suitably prepared, although recent winters have seen fairly extreme snowfall, which effectively shut down the local infrastructure, including public transport, and resulted in enormous snow drifts and obliterated trails.

Although Northumberland National Park and other places on St Cuthbert's Way receive fewer visitors during peak season than the Lake District, the same cannot be said about Holy Island, which in summer can get rather busy.

Some businesses close out of season – Harestanes Visitor Centre, for example, is open April–October, whereas Melrose Abbey and

Lindisfarne Priory are open all year, but with reduced days/hours in the winter. Some B&Bs close for a brief period in November, December or January, but this varies from place to place.

Wildlife and birdlife can be seen throughout the year, although certain species are only present in specific months or seasons. Late spring and summer (May–July) are the best seasons for seabirds on the coast and the Farne Islands; winter migrants arrive in October or November.

Heather moorland is perhaps at its most beautiful in August, and in late autumn deciduous forest will be a kaleidoscope of reds and golds (indeed some would argue that this is the best season to visit one of the most spectacular gardens in the area, at Belsay Hall).

It is worth bearing in mind the dates of the lambing season (April–May) and the grouse season (August–December). Be careful not to disturb livestock in the former; during the latter, some hotels can be booked out by shooting parties.

WHAT TO TAKE

The clothing and equipment you take depends largely on what season you choose to visit, and will be similar to that required for walking in other upland areas of Britain. A waterproof shell (Gore-tex or similar) is mandatory at any time of year, as are layers of warm clothing (lightweight base and mid layers, and a warm/windproof fleece jacket or similar), lightweight trousers, hat and gloves, trekking poles and good quality, comfortable walking boots and socks. Outside the summer months you should bring warmer trousers, and gaiters if walking in winter snow. Maps, compass, sunblock, an emergency 'space' blanket and a whistle for attracting attention, and a small first aid kit (including fabric plasters and stretch bandage for sprains and blisters) are other essentials. Make sure you carry sufficient water and food – while some stages pass villages with shops or pubs, others do not, in which case you will need to carry enough for that day.

WAYMARKING AND ACCESS

The route described in this guide is for the most part clearly marked with a series of distinctive waymarkings displayed on stiles or gateposts, marker poles and signposts and the like. In the few cases where these are not displayed, the trail is clearly marked with public footpath signs.

St Cuthbert's Way is way-marked by a St Cuthbert's Cross. The **Northumberland Coast Path** 'shares' the trail markings of the **England Coast Path** and the **North Sea Trail**.

Other prominent waymarkings you will encounter at certain points on these trails include those of the Pennine Way (an acorn), St Oswald's Way (a raven) and the Border Abbeys Way (an amalgamated 'A' and 'W').

Waymarkings for St Cuthbert's Way and the Northumberland Coast Path

MAPS

St Cuthbert's Way is covered by both the OS Explorer® (1:25,000) and OS Landranger® (1:50,000) series, as follows:

- OS Explorer 338, OL16, 340, with Berwick-upon-Tweed just off the latter on 346; OS Landranger 73, 74, 75.

Harvey's has a map of St Cuthbert's Way (1:40,000), as well as a sheet covering the Cheviots (1:25,000).

All maps in this guide are based on the OS Landranger series (1:50,000). If you want more detail, the OS Explorer sheets are the ones to get.

HILL AND COASTAL SAFETY

The route described in this guide is for the most part fairly low level; however, the Cheviots and other upland areas require the same precautions as any other upland area in the UK. Low cloud can make route finding (which under good weather conditions would be perfectly easy) more challenging, and occasional screaming winds can make it difficult to stand up, let alone walk in a straight line. Some winters have seen extremely heavy snowfall, beginning as early as late November and falling continually for several days, leaving deep drifts in the hills and even on the rocks and beaches of the Northumberland coast, on occasions leaving a carpet of snow some 30cm deep.

Always carry waterproofs and sufficient warm clothing, a torch, first aid kit, whistle (for attracting attention in an emergency), map and compass (and know how to use them) or a GPS, an emergency or 'space' blanket, and adequate water and food. Follow local weather forecasts. Be alert for traffic on sections of road walking – not that there is likely to be much, but country lanes are narrow and sometimes have little in the way of a grass verge to step onto; and when crossing the East Coast Main Line near Fenwick, call the signalbox from the phone provided and wait for clearance (a diversion to bypass this crossing was in place at the time of writing, in 2022, but may become permanent).

TREADING LIGHTLY

- Keep to marked footpaths and other rights of way wherever possible, and avoid increasing erosion or damage to adjacent areas. Sand dunes, heather moorland and peat bogs all constitute fragile ecosystems, easily damaged by even the most well-meaning feet.
- Carry all of your litter with you, and dispose of it responsibly in a town or village.
- Do not pick flowers or disturb wildlife.
- Leave gates as you found them.
- Do not disturb livestock, particularly during the lambing season (April–May).
- Keep dogs on a lead when crossing farmland and during breeding season for ground-nesting birds (April–July).
- Do not light open fires.

It is essential that you check the safe crossing times for the walk across the sands to Holy Island (or for that matter if crossing by road along the causeway). You need to allow at least 1hr to cross the sands from the first refuge box at South Low (the distance from the mainland to South Low then

Refuge box on the Pilgrim's Route across the sands to Holy Island (Stage 5)

Memorial cross in front of the ruins of Lindisfarne Priory, Holy Island (Stage 5)

over the sands to Chare Ends is a little over 2½ miles (4.5km) – some advise allowing up to 2hrs if the sand is soft), and you can only cross the sands safely during the middle of the safe crossing period. Ideally, you should aim to *complete* your crossing by the midpoint of the crossing period. Tides may also be influenced by strong winds and other adverse weather conditions. You are strongly advised not to attempt crossing in the dark; besides the danger posed by the tide, accidentally straying from the correct route potentially carries the (albeit unlikely) hazard of quicksands and unexploded ordnance.

Safe crossing times for Holy Island are available online from Northumberland County Council (go to www.northumberland.gov.uk and enter 'Holy Island causeway safe crossing times' in the search field) and are prominently and very clearly displayed at the entrance to the Holy Island causeway – so there really is no excuse for 'accidentally' crossing outside these times. Nevertheless, the RNLI, usually in conjunction with an RAF helicopter from Boulmer, is still required to make several rescues each year of motorists (and only a very small number of walkers) stranded by the tides while crossing to or from Holy Island.

EMERGENCIES

North of the border, St Cuthbert's Way is covered by the Border Search and Rescue Unit (www.bordersar.org.uk), one of the teams that make up the Mountain Rescue Committee of Scotland (www.scottishmountainrescue.org).

In an emergency **dial 999 or 112** and ask for police, then mountain rescue. Calls are then routed to the police control room in the area of the incident (and if required, to another emergency service such as ambulance service or air ambulance). It is important to provide as much information as possible about the accident, the location and nature of the terrain. Be prepared to give the following information:

- Casualties (number, names, ages if known, type of injuries, plus your name)
- Hazards to the rescuers (such as strong winds, rock fall, dangerous animals)
- Access (name of area and description of terrain, and weather conditions if relevant)
- Location of the incident (ideally a grid reference or GPS reference, otherwise a description including any obvious features; map sheet number if known; and specify whether reference is from a map or a GPS)
- Equipment at the scene (torches, mobile phones, warm clothing, emergency shelters)
- Type of incident (what happened, time and apparent cause of incident).

South of the Scottish border, St Cuthbert's Way falls within the geographical area covered by NESRA (North East Search and Rescue Association, www.nesra. org.uk), one of the nine regional organisations belonging to Mountain Rescue England and Wales (www. mountain.rescue.org.uk). NESRA acts as an umbrella body for the seven local mountain rescue teams across

'The Journey', Fenwick Lawson's wooden sculpture of monks from Lindisfarne carrying the body of St Cuthbert as they flee Viking raids (Stage 5)

33

North East England. The two local teams covering the area relevant to this guidebook are Northumberland National Park Mountain Rescue Team (nnpmrt.org) and North of Tyne Search and Rescue Team (www.notmrt.org.uk); however, in case of emergency do *not* contact the teams directly, dial 999 as described above.

If stranded by the tide or in other emergencies on the Northumberland coast, dial 999 or 112 and ask for the coastguard (www.rnli.org.uk).

USING THIS GUIDE

The guide uses OS mapping, more specifically the Landranger (1:50,000) series. These should be perfectly sufficient for walking these routes, although if you want to explore the area further, the OS Explorer (1:25,000) series is recommended.

Distances in this guide are given in miles as well as kilometres; elevation is given in metres. The route timings given are an estimate based on a walker of average fitness level; timings do not include stops for rest, lunch or visiting sites passed along the routes.

Within the route descriptions R and L are used for right and left, and N, S, SE (and so on) for compass bearings. References to L and R river banks indicate 'true' left and right; in other words, they assume you are looking downstream.

For the sake of brevity, abbreviations have also been used for the main route names in the text, as follows:

- **SCW** St Cuthbert's Way
- **NCP** Northumberland Coast Path
- **ECP** England Coast Path
- **NST** North Sea Trail

For other long-distance footpaths that are only mentioned or encountered briefly (for example, the Border Abbeys Way, St Oswald's Way and the Pennine Way) their full title has been used.

ST CUTHBERT'S WAY

Trail leading up to the border ridge in the Cheviot hills, where St Cuthbert's Way crosses from the Borders into Northumberland (Stage 3)

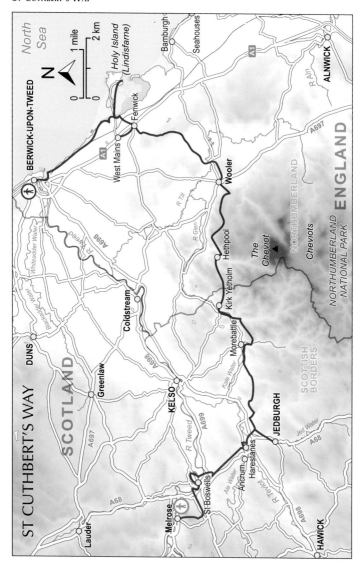

INTRODUCTION

Boot scraper in woods near Monteviot House (Stage 2)

St Cuthbert's Way was opened in 1996, its route covering a distance of 62 miles (100km) from Melrose, in the Borders, to Holy Island (Lindisfarne) on the north Northumberland coast. The route links several sites associated with the life of the seventh-century St Cuthbert: Melrose Abbey, of which St Cuthbert was prior; St Cuthbert's Cave, where monks fleeing from Lindisfarne carrying the saint's body and other relics stopped to rest; and Holy Island itself, where St Cuthbert was prior and later bishop. The walk, which is divided roughly equally between the Borders and Northumberland, visits three of the great Border abbeys and several unspoilt villages, before crossing the Cheviots and winding through more history-studded landscape to the Northumberland Coast.

In this guide there are a few slight changes to the standard breakdown of stages of St Cuthbert's Way. Firstly, in the conventional route, the first stage finishes at Harestanes, but there is no accommodation here – necessitating a detour to nearby Ancrum or Jedburgh. For this reason, in this guide the first stage has been extended into Jedburgh (which has far more accommodation available than Ancrum, and gives walkers a chance to visit the magnificent

Jedburgh Abbey) along a section of the Border Abbeys Way. Secondly, the short detour to Dryburgh Abbey is here treated as an integral part of the route. Thirdly, walkers are advised to consider stopping at West Mains rather than walking from Wooler to Holy Island in one day, since crossing to Holy Island is dependent on tides and safe crossing times, and is thus not always possible in the evening (see 'Hill and coastal safety').

The standard route description for St Cuthbert's Way is usually spread over four days, and it shares some of its route in Scotland with the Border Abbeys Way and the Pennine Way, and some of its final stages in Northumberland with St Oswald's Way and the Northumberland Coast Path.

For reference, the 'standard' Melrose–Holy Island route is usually described as follows:

- **Stage 1** Melrose to Harestanes – 15 miles (24km)
- **Stage 2** Harestanes to Kirk Yetholm – 16½ miles (27km)
- **Stage 3** Kirk Yetholm to Wooler – 13 miles (21km)
- **Stage 4** Wooler to Holy Island – 16½ miles (27km)

In this guide, the route is described as continuing from Holy Island up the coast to Berwick-upon-Tweed – an additional 11½ miles (18.5km) – following the Northumberland Coast Path. This avoids a walk back along the road to West Mains, and allows walkers to take advantage of the better transport links from Berwick. Just as importantly, the extended walk passes through some of the most beautiful coastal scenery in Britain. This increases the length of the route to 77½ miles (125km), which would best be spread over six days.

A summary of the stages described here is as follows:

- **Stage 1** Melrose to Jedburgh – 19½ miles (32km)
- **Stage 2** Jedburgh to Kirk Yetholm – 16 miles (26km)
- **Stage 3** Kirk Yetholm to Wooler – 13 miles (21km)
- **Stage 4** Wooler to West Mains – 13 miles (21.5km)
- **Stage 5** West Mains to Holy Island – 6 miles (9.5km)
- **Stage 6** Holy Island to Berwick-upon-Tweed – 11½ miles (18.5km)

For those who want to follow the route at a more leisurely pace, the following breakdown of stages is recommended:

- **Stage 1** Melrose to St Boswell's – 7½ miles (12km)
- **Stage 2** St Boswell's to Jedburgh – 12 miles (19.5km)
- **Stage 3** Jedburgh to Morebattle – 9½ miles (15km)
- **Stage 4** Morebattle to Kirk Yetholm – 6½ miles (11km)

View over the River Tweed to the Eildon Hills, from near Dryburgh Abbey (Stage 1)

- **Stage 5** Kirk Yetholm to Hethpool – 5 miles (8km)
- **Stage 6** Hethpool to Wooler – 8 miles (13km)
- **Stage 7** Wooler to West Mains – 13 miles (21.5km)
- **Stage 8** West Mains to Holy Island – 6 miles (9.5km)
- **Stage 9** Holy Island to Berwick-upon-Tweed – 11½ miles (18.5km)

There is plenty of accommodation in Jedburgh and Wooler, slightly less at Kirk Yetholm. As mentioned previously, there is no accommodation at Harestanes. Stopping in West Mains has the advantage of being close to Holy Island, making it easy to visit as a day trip. There are also several places to stay at intermediate points on the route, including St Boswell's.

STAGE 1
Melrose to Jedburgh

Start	Melrose Abbey, Melrose
Finish	Jedburgh Abbey, Jedburgh
Distance	19½ miles (32km)
Time	8hr 15min
Maps	OS Explorer 338 and OL16; OS Landranger 73
Access	Bus 60 or 67 from Berwick-upon-Tweed to Melrose; bus X95 from Carlisle or Edinburgh to Galashiels or X62 from Edinburgh to Galashiels, then bus 61 from Galashiels to Melrose
Accommodation	Station Hotel and several other choices in Melrose; Glenbank House Hotel and several alternatives in Jedburgh. Accommodation also available in St Boswells and (more limited and with a detour) near Ancrum

This is an easy – although long – stage that takes in a wealth of historical and scenic interest, including the abbeys at Melrose, Dryburgh and Jedburgh, Roman Dere Street, the Eildon Hills and the River Tweed. There are good paths with some road walking, and a short, steep climb over the Eildons. If preferred, this stage can conveniently be broken into two stages by stopping at St Boswells.

The route description and timings include a visit to the superbly atmospheric Dryburgh Abbey, just off the main route of SCW before St Boswells.

This first stage is usually described as finishing at Harestanes; however, as there is no accommodation there this effectively means a detour to Ancrum, a 1-mile (1.5km) road walk (but accommodation there is very limited), or continuing to Jedburgh, as described here. Alternatively, you could take a bus (number 68) from Ancrum to Jedburgh, and return by bus in the morning.

From **Melrose Abbey**, follow the road S to the market square, then straight ahead up Dingleton Road and under the flyover carrying the A68. Turn L down a flight of steps signposted Eildon Walk and SCW, then ascend a steep path (which can be slippery after rain) with occasional

MELROSE

The Church of St Mary the Virgin at Melrose Abbey (search for 'Melrose Abbey' on www.historicenvironment.scot) was founded in 1136, although much of it dates from the late 14th century, after it was largely destroyed by an army led by Richard II in 1385. It is a magnificent building, rich in sculptural detail, from saints to gargoyles, courtiers and demons – look out for the bagpipe-playing pig on the south exterior walls of the church. The church is thought to be the burial place of Robert the Bruce's heart, and is also the final resting place of the Scottish King Alexander II. It is worth climbing the stairs to the rooftop, both for the view of the abbey itself and of the Eildon Hills to the south, which our route crosses after leaving Melrose.

Old Melrose, thought to have been the site of the monastery during St Cuthbert's lifetime, lies about 2½ miles (4km) east of town. The site of Trimontium, a large Roman military camp, lies just east of Melrose at Newstead, and there is a small museum in the Ormiston Institute on the main square in Melrose itself (www.trimontium.co.uk). According to legend, King Arthur lies buried somewhere in the nearby Eildon Hills – although there is of course no evidence for this. Along the minor road leading southeast from Melrose over the flanks of the Eildons is the Rhymer's Stone, a memorial to the 13th-century Thomas the Rhymer, credited with prophecy. Abbotsford, the former home of the poet and novelist Sir Walter Scott, lies just to the west of Melrose. Also in Melrose are Priorwood Garden and Harmony Garden (search for both on www.nts.org.uk). Melrose is also the birthplace of seven-a-side rugby, and hosts the annual Melrose Sevens in April. If you are in Melrose in June, your visit may coincide with the Borders Book Festival (www.bordersbookfestival.org).

The ruins of the 12th-century Melrose Abbey

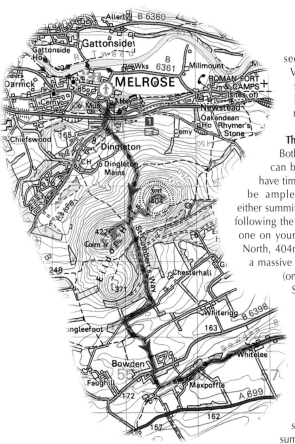

sections of steps. Veer R to gain a saddle (320m) between the two main **Eildon Hills**.

The Eildon Hills

Both the main **Eildons** can be climbed if you have time (15mins should be ample time to reach either summit from the saddle, following the clear paths). The one on your left (Eildon Hill North, 404m) is crowned by a massive Iron Age hill **fort** (one of the largest in Scotland). It was once a stronghold of the Votadini tribe until they were conquered by the Romans, following which it was the site of a Roman signal station. The summit on your right (Mid Eildon, 422m) is the highest, and has a view indicator at its summit **cairn**. The views from either summit are excellent, with the Cheviots to the south and the Lammermuirs to the north. You should also be able to pick out the line of Dere Street, the Roman road followed by SCW in the second half of this stage.

Map continues on page 44

Follow the path down the other side from the saddle, joining a track and bearing L (the path on the R is to the third, lower Eildon). Go L through a gate and into

woodland, then veer R. Where the track turns R just before the edge of the wood, keep straight ahead then follow a path along the edge of the trees. Turn L and descend, crossing a farm track, then ascend steps through a plantation to arrive in the village of **Bowden**. There is a prominent octagonal stone well by the road here.

Crossing the Eildon Hills, near Melrose

Turn R onto the road, then turn L onto a road signposted for SCW and Bowden Kirk. Turn L onto a path where the road veers R. Bowden Kirk can be visited as a short detour, by following the road to the R. ▶ Cross the bridge to the other side of the **Bowden Burn** and turn L, following the true R bank. The path climbs to a track that runs above the valley of the Bowden Burn, and after a short distance you will notice an old stone bridge below you on your L, on what must have been the course of the old road to Bowden.

There has been a church at this site since the 12th century, although the present building dates mostly from the 17th–18th centuries.

When the track reaches **Whitelee**, continue straight ahead on the road, passing under a **disused railway line** before arriving at **Newton St Boswells**. Cross the A68 and continue on the road straight ahead, then turn L following signs for SCW, the Border Abbeys Way and the river. Descend under the bridge carrying the A68 then continue on a path, crossing a bridge over a stream. Bear

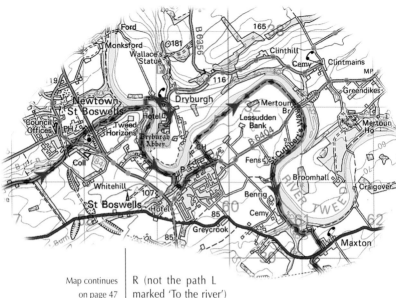

Map continues
on page 47

R (not the path L
marked 'To the river')
then climb steps to gain a path above the **River Tweed**,
with an excellent viewpoint looking back towards the
Eildons. Follow the path down to the Tweed and the
Dryburgh Suspension Bridge, built in 1872.

> The **River Tweed** stretches some 97 miles (156km)
> across southern Scotland and Northumberland,
> rising at Tweed's Well near Foal Burn Head and Bog
> Hill, and emptying into the North Sea at Berwick-
> upon-Tweed. It is internationally known for its
> fishing, in particular Atlantic salmon – more of
> which are caught here than on any other river in the
> UK. The Tweed and its catchment rivers have been
> designated an SSSI.

Cross the bridge (note the small classical Temple of the
Muses on the far side) and turn R, passing a magnificent
sandstone gateway on your L (built by the 11th Earl of
Buchan in the early 19th century, as the entrance to his
orchard), to reach **Dryburgh Abbey** in about 10min.

44

Now a romantic ruin tucked into a bend of the River Tweed, **Dryburgh Abbey** was founded in 1150 by Hugh de Moreville, Constable of Scotland, who invited canons of the Premonstratensian Order from Alnwick in Northumberland. It grew into the main Premonstratensian foundation in Scotland, but was attacked and burnt by English forces several times in the 14th and 16th centuries. The final blow came in 1544 when it was torched, along with much of the rest of Dryburgh, by the Earl of Hertford, and the Reformation finally sealed its fate in 1560. In 1786 it was purchased by David Steuart Erskine, 11th Earl of Buchan, who moved into nearby Dryburgh House. The North Transept Chapel contains the tomb of Sir Walter Scott. For those who wish to stay in Dryburgh, there is the Dryburgh Abbey Hotel (www.dryburgh.co.uk, tel 01835 822261).

Just north of the village is an enormous sandstone statue of Scottish national hero William Wallace, carved in the early 19th century.

Return to the true R bank of the Tweed and follow the path alongside a bend in the river. After going up and down several sections of wooden steps, turn R and ascend to the village of **St Boswells**. There is a low section of the path here that is prone to flooding after very heavy rainfall. ▸

If there is flooding, follow the road W from the Dryburgh Suspension Bridge and turn L onto the A68, which will take you into St Boswells.

St Boswells was an important centre by the 16th century, although much of it was razed to the ground by the English army in 1544. The surprisingly large village green (known simply as The Green), thought to be the largest in Scotland, is home to an annual livestock fair dating back to the 1600s. This began as a week-long sheep fair, but had become a one-day event (including large numbers of horses and cattle) by the early 19th century. St Boswell's Fair is held on 18 July. The name St Boswells appears to derive from St Boisil,

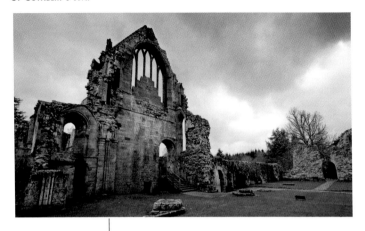

The ruins of Dryburgh Abbey

a monk from Melrose Abbey who was an early mentor of St Cuthbert.

Accommodation is available at the Buccleuch Arms Hotel (www.buccleucharms.com, tel 01835 822243) and the Dryburgh Arms (https://dryburgharms.co.uk). The 67 bus stops in St Boswells.

Smailholm Tower, a well-preserved 15th-century tower house, is only some 4 miles (6.5km) northeast of St Boswells. From the 17th century, Smailholm Tower, and later the adjacent Sandyknowe, were owned by the Scott family, and it was here that Sir Walter Scott spent part of his childhood recovering from illness.

From the village green in St Boswells, walk E along the main road (B6404) as far as Braeheads Road, opposite a prominent drinking fountain. Turn L onto Braeheads Road, then bear R and follow the edge of the golf course alongside the River Tweed. After passing an area of eroded sandstone on the far bank, cross the road next to the **Mertoun Bridge** (which dates from the 19th century), and continue alongside the river and into woodland. After the cemetery you pass Maxton Church, which is dedicated to St Cuthbert

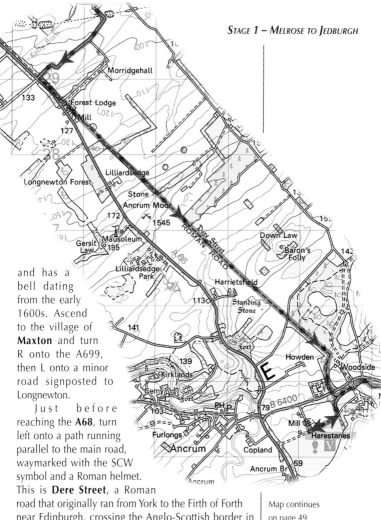

and has a bell dating from the early 1600s. Ascend to the village of **Maxton** and turn R onto the A699, then L onto a minor road signposted to Longnewton.

Just before reaching the **A68**, turn left onto a path running parallel to the main road, waymarked with the SCW symbol and a Roman helmet. This is **Dere Street**, a Roman road that originally ran from York to the Firth of Forth near Edinburgh, crossing the Anglo-Scottish border in the Cheviots near the source of the River Coquet. It was probably constructed around AD80. Initially a path through trees and alongside fields, Dere Street later becomes a broad grassy expanse between two fences, passing Lilliard's Stone on the R.

Map continues on page 49

47

Lilliard's Stone is a small monument to a woman who, according to legend, fought bravely in the Battle of Ancrum Moor, which was fought between the Scots and the English near this spot in 1545. There was once a large cross here, erected by the monks of Melrose Abbey, and in the late 14th century representatives of the English and Scottish crowns would come here to attempt to resolve disputes. Beyond Lilliard's Stone and clearly visible on Gersit Law, on the far side of the A68, is the mausoleum of General Sir Thomas Monteath Douglas.

On the horizon ahead of you as you follow Dere Street is the **Waterloo Monument**, a huge 150ft (46m) tower on Peniel Heugh, visible for miles around. It was completed in 1824, after an earlier version of the monument had collapsed. You also pass a lake and wetland area known as Baron's Folly Moss on your left, which has plenty of birdlife. ◄

The lake takes its name from the small building on top of Down Law, Baron's Folly, said to have been built by an unknown baron as a secret meeting place for himself and his lover.

Cross a minor road and enter woodland, passing a trail on the R to Woodside Gardens, a Victorian walled garden and tea room that is only a few minutes away (www.woodside garden.co.uk). Cross another road, then follow the path over a wooden bridge and turn R off the main trail towards Harestanes, about 5min further on.

Harestanes Visitor Centre, a former farm, has exhibitions and events, a gift shop, tea room, nature trail and a large outdoor children's play area (01835 830306, open April–September). The Waterloo Monument can be reached on foot from Harestanes, although the tower itself is not open to the public.

There is currently no accommodation at Harestanes and only very limited options in nearby Ancrum, so unless you're being picked up at Harestanes or plan to take a bus into Jedburgh, you'll need to continue walking to Jedburgh as follows.

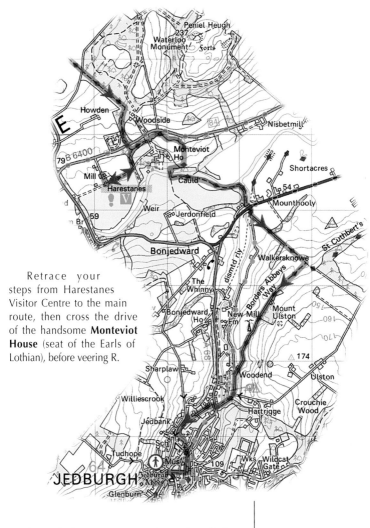

Retrace your steps from Harestanes Visitor Centre to the main route, then cross the drive of the handsome **Monteviot House** (seat of the Earls of Lothian), before veering R.

Monteviot House (www.monteviot.com) was built in 1740, and partially enlarged in the 19th century by the architect Edward Blore (who also worked on Buckingham Palace). The gardens are open to the public during the summer (April–October).

19th-century dovecote in woods near Monteviot House

Turn R again before the **River Teviot**, passing a sign to 'river view' on your L. Look out for the boot scraper next to a tree, and the large 19th-century dovecote, both on your L. The path moves away from the river for a short section, before turning L to reach the suspension bridge, built in 1999 after an earlier bridge was damaged by floods. It is apt to sway a little uncomfortably in the wind. Turn L and follow the river bank, turning R just before reaching the Jed Water, which you follow to the **A698**.

Turn L and follow the main road across the bridge, then take the road on your R. Bear L and follow the track uphill, with good views back to Peniel Heugh and the Waterloo Monument. Just over ½ mile (1km) after leaving the A698 you reach a junction with the Border Abbeys Way trail on your R. Turn R onto the Border Abbeys Way, and L onto the minor road before reaching the Jed Water and the A68. Cross the main road with care and follow the river path (or simply turn L and follow the main road itself) into the centre of **Jedburgh**.

JEDBURGH

Jedburgh first appears in documents in AD864, when a bishop of Lindisfarne established two settlements on the Jed Water, both called Gedwearde. It was sacked or occupied repeatedly over the centuries by English armies as they passed this way – eventually, the Scots destroyed the castle themselves rather than have it keep falling into English hands. Locals often pronounce Jedburgh as 'Jeddart'.

Jedburgh Abbey was founded by David I in 1138, as a priory for canons of the Augustinian order, who had perhaps come from St Quentin Abbey in France. It is exceptionally well preserved (especially when one considers its position so close to the 'troubled' English–Scottish border), with much of the Abbey Church of St Mary the Virgin still standing after almost 900 years. The Abbey Visitor Centre has a good collection of artefacts, including an ivory comb from around 1100 (search for 'Jedburgh Abbey' on www.historicenvironment.scot).

Other places to visit while in Jedburgh include the fortified house in which Mary Queen of Scots stayed in 1566. She fell seriously ill during

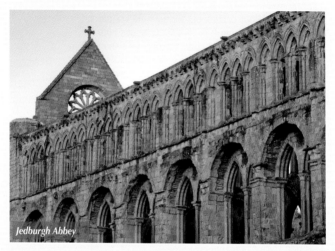
Jedburgh Abbey

her stay, and is said to have commented later when locked in the Tower of London, 'Would that I had died in Jedburgh!'

James Hutton, often considered the father of modern geology, was born in Jedburgh. The distinctive rock formations at nearby Inchbonny – vertical and folded bands of rock surmounted by horizontal bands of sandstone – are among those which led him to challenge conventional notions of geological time in his book *Theory of the Earth* (1788). Inchbonny can be reached by walking south a short distance from the town centre on the A68.

Accommodation in Jedburgh includes the Royal Hotel (www.royal hoteljedburgh.com, tel 01835 863152) and Meadhon House B&B (www.meadhon.co.uk, tel 01835 862504).

STAGE 2
Jedburgh to Kirk Yetholm

Start	Jedburgh Abbey, Jedburgh
Finish	Village green, Kirk Yetholm
Distance	16 miles (26km)
Time	7hr 45min
Maps	OS Explorer OL16; OS Landranger 74
Access	Bus 51 Jedburgh–Edinburgh; 68 Jedburgh–Galashiels
Accommodation	The Farmhouse at Yetholm Mill; a few alternatives in Kirk Yetholm and Town Yetholm. Accommodation is also available in Morebattle

This moderate stage of the walk crosses Wideopen Hill, the highest point on SCW, on the edge of the Cheviots and with breathtaking views, with good paths and two fairly long stretches of road walking. If preferred, this stage can be broken with a stop at Morebattle.

Map continues on page 54

Retrace your steps from **Jedburgh** along the Border Abbeys Way to the junction with SCW, turn R (SE), then almost immediately take the marked path on the L, leaving Roman Dere Street at this point. The trail passes through attractive woodland, with silver birch and other trees. Turn R at the road, then keep straight ahead on a track where the road veers R. Descend to

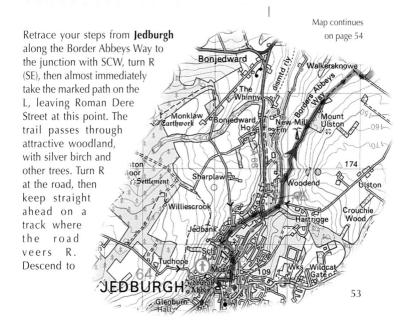

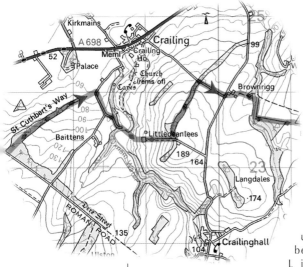

the bridge over the **Oxnam Water**, near prominent sandstone cliffs, then continue up the slope beyond. Pass the farmhouses at the top, then keep straight ahead up the road, before turning L into a narrow sliver of woodland just before the top of the hill. Turn R onto a road again, passing **Brownrigg Farm** and continuing alongside fields and through patches of woodland.

About 4½ miles (7km) after the junction of SCW and the Border Abbeys Way, turn L onto a farm track, soon veering R with excellent views ahead to the ruins of Cessford Castle and the Cheviots beyond. This brings you

The ruins of Cessford Castle, near Morebattle, built in the 15th century

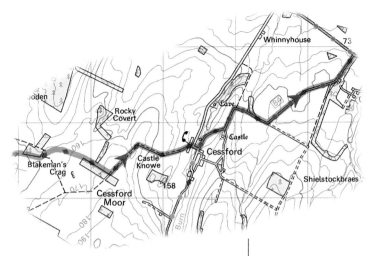

to **Cessford**, with its pretty row of houses built in 1870. Before this date Cessford was actually a much larger and more important settlement, but following the Enclosure Acts of the late 18th and early 19th centuries, many of the smaller houses were demolished. On reaching the sealed road, head over the bridge, then follow the road around to the L, to reach **Cessford Castle** on your R. Walk up across the field for a better view (but do not enter the building, since the masonry is unstable).

Map continues on page 56

Dating from the mid-15th century (although there was possibly already some form of castle here at least a century earlier), **Cessford Castle** was a stronghold of the Kers, one of the most powerful families in the area. It is a massive and uncompromising structure, clearly built with defence a paramount consideration (the border with England lies only 8 miles/13 km away) – the walls are over 13ft (around 4m) thick in places. During the 1500s it was besieged several times by the English, and the Kers were also embroiled in an ongoing blood feud with another powerful clan, the Scotts of Buccleuch. The castle was abandoned in 1607.

55

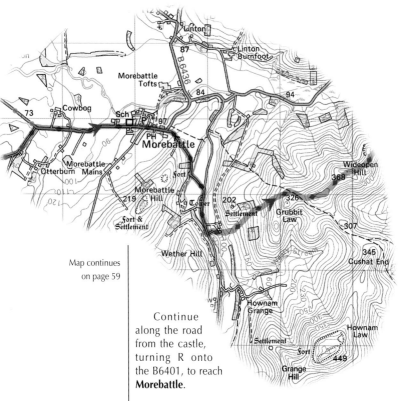

Map continues
on page 59

Continue along the road from the castle, turning R onto the B6401, to reach **Morebattle**.

Morebattle is a small village by the Kale Water, at the foot of the Cheviots. The church dates mostly from the 18th century, with later additions from 1899. An earlier church on this site was destroyed by fire in 1544. The name Morebattle means 'settlement by the lake', referring to Linton Loch, a large area of marshland to the northeast between Morebattle and Linton, which was drained in the 18th century (a small remnant of this still exists below the north flanks of Wideopen Hill, where the B6401 heads over towards Yetholm). Meals and accommodation in Morebattle are available at the Templehall Inn (www.templehallhotel.com, tel 01573 440249).

According to legend, the nearby village of Linton was the abode of the so-called **Linton Worm**, a medieval dragon (slain by one John de Somerville). The legend bears similarities to that other famous 'worm' of the northeast, the Lambton Worm, upon which Bram Stoker's novel *The Lair of the White Worm* is based.

The route over Grubbit Law and Wideopen Hill between Morebattle and Kirk Yetholm

Head E through the centre of Morebattle, passing the **Templehall Inn** on the R, then taking the smaller road up on your R, with the knobbly hills of the Cheviots ahead. Descend on a road to your L, then turn R onto the road alongside the **Kale Water**. An old tower is just visible, hidden in the trees to your R. Pass a ford on your L, then shortly after this turn L and cross the stream on the wooden footbridge.

The Cheviots are the remnants of a massive granite intrusion injected into the earth's crust beneath the volcanoes that stood here some 360 million years ago. Heat generated by the superheated granite of this intrusion hardened the existing

A view of the Cheviots (with Hownam Law on the right), from the route over Wideopen Hill

lava with which it came into contact, and the resulting metamorphosed rock, now eroded, forms a series of rocky tors. Vegetation on the Cheviots is characterised by hardy moor grass, rather than heather. The highest peak, The Cheviot (804m), lies around 5½ miles (9km) south of SCW, just east of the border ridge.

Follow the farm track as it zigzags uphill, then turn R onto a footpath that ascends between two small areas of woodland. The path continues to climb steeply, bringing you just to the L (N) of **Grubbit Law** (326m) and crossing a footpath that heads over Cushat End (345m) to the SE. Head more or less NE over open, blustery tops, with patches of heather moorland bringing splashes of colour to the surrounding hills. The views to the R (SE) are particularly impressive. The striking and very prominent, almost flat-topped hill to the SE is Hownam Law (449m), site of an Iron Age hill fort.

Follow the trail alongside a stone wall to reach **Wideopen Hill** (368m), which marks both the highest point on St Cuthbert's Way, and the approximate midway point between Melrose and Lindisfarne.

Follow the wall round to the R, then L. Descend steeply (slippery after rain), then ascend slightly, and walk alongside another wall over **Crookedshaws Hill** (306m), before descending steeply again. Turn R then L through fields to arrive at a track. Turn R onto this and follow it down to the road, which you turn L onto. After ¾ mile

(1km) you come to the **B6401**, which you follow for a further ¾ mile (1km) into **Town Yetholm**, passing The Plough Hotel; turn R and cross the bridge to reach **Kirk Yetholm**.

To reach The Farmhouse B&B, keep straight ahead and you will find it on your L; to reach the Border Hotel, either continue up the road beyond The Farmhouse B&B, or take the signed SCW path from just after the bridge, in either case arriving at the village green and the hotel in 5min.

KIRK YETHOLM

The history of Kirk Yetholm is closely associated with that of the Scottish Gypsies (in particular the Faa family), who had settled here by the end of the 17th century. One theory of their arrival in Yetholm is that they were granted the right to settle here by Sir William Bennet of Marlfield, as a reward for service in the late 17th or

Monument to the Yetholm Gypsies, next to the village green in Kirk Yetholm

early 18th century – although their presence in Scotland goes back at least to the 16th century.

The village green lies at the northern end of the Pennine Way. An unusual feature of Kirk (and Town) Yetholm is the presence of a number of thatched cottages, which are not generally found in this area.

Accommodation in Kirk Yetholm includes The Farmhouse B&B (www.thefarmhouseatkirkyetholm.com, tel 01573 420505) and The Border Hotel (www.borderhotel.co.uk, tel 01573 420237) – both excellent – as well as the Friends of Nature House Hostel (https://friendsofnature.org.uk/houses/kirk-yetholm, tel 01573 420639); while in Town Yetholm there is The Plough Hotel (www.theploughhotelyetholm.co.uk, tel 01573 420215).

STAGE 3
Kirk Yetholm to Wooler

Start	Village green, Kirk Yetholm
Finish	High Street, Wooler
Distance	13 miles (21km)
Time	6hr 40min
Maps	OS Explorer OL16; OS Landranger 74 and 75
Access	Bus 81 (Mon–Sat) Kelso–Yetholm
Accommodation	The Tankerville Arms and several alternatives in Wooler; limited accommodation available at Hethpool and (off-route) in the College Valley

This is a reasonably short but fairly strenuous stage spent almost entirely in the Cheviots, crossing the border ridge between Kirk Yetholm and Hethpool, then climbing to more high ground between Yeavering Bell and the Newton Tors. There are good paths, magnificent scenery and around 600m of ascent. It can be broken into two stages by stopping at or just beyond Hethpool.

From the village green in **Kirk Yetholm** take the road uphill signposted to Halterburn, SCW now sharing its route with that of the Pennine Way.

Map continues on page 63

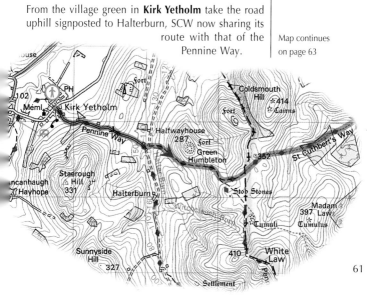

Border fence between England and Scotland

Turn L off the road at the bottom of the hill, crossing the **Halter Burn** and ascending steadily on a clear trail. About ¾ mile (1km) after leaving the road, the trail veers L, leaving the Pennine Way which continues straight ahead. Coninue uphill to the border fence and wall, where twin signs pointing in opposite directions announce 'Welcome to Scotland' and 'Welcome to England'. Cross the stile, casting your eye back for a last look at the way you have come. Then say farewell to Scotland and step into Northumberland.

Follow the trail straight ahead, ascending slightly – from where a short detour to Eccles Cairn (352m), on your L, gives further enhanced views – then descending, through several boggy patches, to reach a plantation. Walk through and along the edge of the plantation (which is surprisingly dark inside), to arrive at a farm track a short distance after emerging from the trees. Follow the farm track to **Elsdonburn Farm**, turning L between the house and outbuildings and crossing the **Elsdon Burn** by a bridge. Turn R onto a sealed road and follow this down the valley, passing one road on the R. Note the cultivation terraces on the L, on the slopes of White Hill, which may be prehistoric in origin. Turn R onto a pretty tree-lined lane and stroll into the tiny village of **Hethpool**.

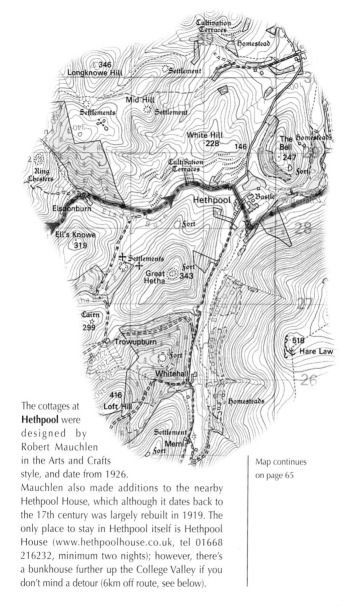

The cottages at **Hethpool** were designed by Robert Mauchlen in the Arts and Crafts style, and date from 1926. Mauchlen also made additions to the nearby Hethpool House, which although it dates back to the 17th century was largely rebuilt in 1919. The only place to stay in Hethpool itself is Hethpool House (www.hethpoolhouse.co.uk, tel 01668 216232, minimum two nights); however, there's a bunkhouse further up the College Valley if you don't mind a detour (6km off route, see below).

Map continues on page 65

Cottages at Hethpool in the College Valley

Stretching south from Hethpool to The Cheviot is the tranquil **College Valley**, a beautiful and remote area owned and managed by the Sir James Knott Trust. It is an area rich in prehistoric remains, including several hill forts and, just south of Hethpool on the west side of the valley, a Neolithic stone circle. Wildlife in the valley includes feral goats (around 150 of them) and red squirrels. The black grouse was reintroduced successfully a few years back, although recently numbers seem to be in decline. The mountains around the head of the valley still bear the remains of several plane crashes from World War 2, where aircraft struck the hillsides during bad weather and poor visibility – several of the survivors were rescued by local shepherds. At Mounthooly, in a wonderful spot near the head of the valley (off route, around 6km south of Hethpool and SCW) there is a bunkhouse (Mounthooly Bunkhouse, www.college-valley. co.uk/accommodation/bunk-house, tel 01668 216210).

Follow the marked track through a field in front of the cottages, crossing a bridge over the **College Burn** and

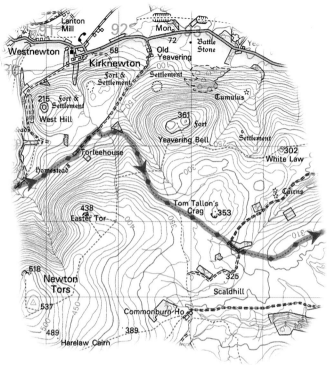

turning L before entering a plantation. As you emerge from the trees, the path crosses a lovely area of moorland with views of Newton Tors on the R and the gorse and scree-covered slopes of The Bell on your L, and Yeavering Bell ahead. ▶ There is a short section of narrow, sometimes slippery path above a stream, which the trail then crosses.

Map continues on page 68

A path on the L leads down to Hethpool Linn waterfall, a 5min detour.

Around this area and on the slopes of the surrounding hills, you may see **feral goats**, which have inhabited this part of the Cheviots for some 150 years. These rather shaggy, long-horned animals were the original domesticated goat in the UK, and would have been kept during the Anglo-Saxon period and earlier, but from the 19th century onwards were gradually replaced by imported breeds, and are now comparatively rare. Herds

The landscape below the Newton Tors, near Hethpool

like this one in the Cheviot Hills almost certainly descend from animals released from captivity in the 19th century.

Pass **Torleehouse Farm** Hethpool, the trail skirting above the farmhouse before joining the gravel farm track just beyond it. Follow this for a short distance then turn R just before a cattle grid, and follow the path uphill and then L. ◄

The trail ascends gradually, crosses a stile and then continues uphill with a wall on the R.

Continuing along the farm track from Torleehouse brings you to Ad Gefrin, the seventh-century palace of the Anglo-Saxon kings of Northumbria.

On your L is the bronze-coloured bulk of **Yeavering Bell** (361m), across the twin summits of which lie the remains of the largest and most important hill fort in Northumberland. Dating from the Iron Age, the site consists of the remains of a massive enclosing wall surrounding an area of some 5.5ha, with numerous circular depressions marking the locations of former buildings.

Pass a trail on the L to Yeavering Bell, then veer L, passing the prominent rocks of **Tom Tallon's Crag** (353m) on your L. The wall that you reach soon after this is said to have been built from the stones of a Bronze Age cairn in the 19th century. Pass a small plantation on your L, joining a track briefly before crossing a small stream and continuing on a path across open moorland. On meeting another wall, turn L and continue alongside it roughly ENE. Veer L and then R, passing **Gains Law** (319m) and **Humbleton Hill** (298m) on your L, and a series of sheepfolds.

Humbleton Hill and the area just south of Gains Law, known as the Trows, provide some of the best examples of sub-glacial meltwater channels in northern England, for which reason they have been listed as an SSSI. Humbleton Hill was itself the site of an Iron Age hill fort. The Battle of Humbleton Hill – mentioned in the opening scene of Shakespeare's *Henry IV Part I* – was fought between the English (under Henry Percy, also known as 'Harry Hotspur') and the Scots in 1402 just north of here.

Yeavering Bell in the Cheviot Hills, site of the largest Iron Age hill fort in Northumberland

Descend further, with the town of Wooler spread out below you, then enter an area of woodland. Head down through the trees to emerge onto one of the educational trails of **Wooler Common**. Turn R to the car park and information boards (the road on the L, Common Road, would also lead you down into Wooler), then veer R alongside a small stream with a plantation on your L. At the corner of the plantation, go through a gate (no waymarkings) onto open moorland, then bear L to reach the far corner of the plantation. Follow the path through the trees, then descend over more open heath, bearing R and passing through a boggy area before reaching the unsealed road by **Waud House**. Follow this down to the houses on the western edge of town, descending Common Road then Ramsey Lane to reach the High Street in **Wooler**.

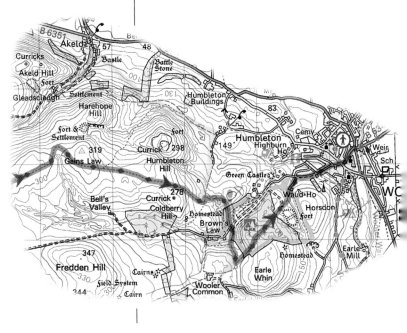

WOOLER

Often described as the gateway to the Cheviots, Wooler is a traditional old market town with 18th- and 19th-century housing clustered in the valley below Humbleton Hill. The remains of the castle lie off Church Street, near a war memorial. The Youth Hostel, just south of the High Street, was purpose built in 1943 to house the local WLA (Women's Land Army), formed to provide agricultural labour following conscription of male farmworkers into the armed forces in World War 2.

The author Virginia Woolf and her husband, Leonard, stayed here for a month in 1914 (lodging at the Tankerville Arms). Leonard commented, 'I am inclined to think that the Cheviots are the loveliest country in England… There is an extraordinary stillness and peace in their forms; and nowhere in the world is the light and colour of sky and earth more lovely than in this bit of England.' Fair praise.

There are shops and pubs in the High Street; the Tankerville Arms (www. tankervillehotel.co.uk, tel 01668 281581), a landmark old coaching inn, is diagonally across the A697 at the bottom of Ryecroft Way (which leads off the northern end of the High Street). There's also a youth hostel in Wooler (www.yha.org.uk/hostel/yha-wooler). The 267 and 464 buses to Berwick-upon-Tweed depart from Wooler.

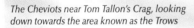

The Cheviots near Tom Tallon's Crag, looking down towards the area known as the Trows

STAGE 4

Wooler to West Mains

Start	High Street, Wooler
Finish	Lindesfarne Inn, West Mains
Distance	13 miles (21.5km)
Time	5hr 25min
Maps	OS Explorer 340; OS Landranger 75
Access	The 267 and 464 Berwick-upon-Tweed–Wooler buses
Accommodation	The Lindisfarne Inn at West Mains; limited options at Beal

With paths, tracks and some road walking, this is an easy stage, which crosses Weetwood Moor and visits St Cuthbert's Cave, before descending towards the coast through Shiellow Wood.

From **Wooler** High Street, descend Church Street, passing St Mary's Church (18th century) and the war memorial, and cross the A697. Cross the bridge over Wooler Water and turn R along a street that follows the course of the dismantled Alnwick–Cornhill Railway.

> The **Alnwick–Cornhill Railway** was a 36-mile (58km), single-track line, opened in 1887. Unable to compete with increasing local bus services, it closed to passengers in the 1930s, although it remained in operation for freight until 1965. The station at Wooler has been converted into two private houses, the trackbed between the platforms having been filled up to platform level. The goods shed is on the A697, just north of the junction with Church Street, and is now an antiques market.

If the lions on the gateposts look rather Venetian, that is because they were made by Italian POWs, when this was a World War 2 prison camp.

Turn L onto Brewery Road, passing a school on your L. ◄ Follow the road uphill then take the marked footpath on your L, with good views back over Wooler, nestled below the Cheviots. The trail now crosses the attractive open moorland of **Weetwood Moor**.

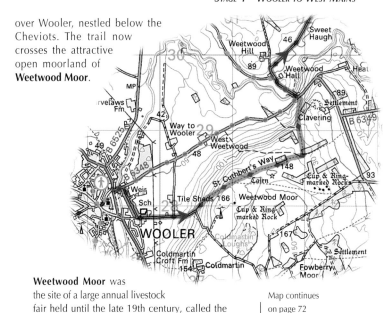

Weetwood Moor was the site of a large annual livestock fair held until the late 19th century, called the

Map continues on page 72

Wooler on the edge of the Cheviot Hills, viewed from the trail to Weetwood Moor

71

*Weetwood bridge,
dating from the
16th century*

Whitsun Tryst (from which the area is gets its local name of Whitsun Bank). There are also several prehistoric sites on Weetwood Moor, including stones with cup-and-ring marks. Some of the cup-and-ring-marked stones can be visited by veering right where the path forks.

Veer L where the path splits into two, passing a small plantation on your L. Turn L through a gate just before reaching a second plantation, then pass another plantation on your L, with excellent views of the Till Valley and the attractive Weetwood
Bridge. Descend

Map continues
on page 75

towards the bridge, taking the R of two paths, and cross
the road carefully. The bridge dates from the 16th century
and was restored in the 18th century, then again in 2005.

Cross the bridge and follow the road uphill, passing
Weetwood Hall, then following the road as it bends around
to the R. North of here is Doddington Moor, an area rich
in prehistoric remains, including numerous cup-and-ring-
marked rocks and the remains of a stone circle and several
settlements. According to local legend, St Cuthbert tended
sheep in this area during his childhood. As you follow the
road NE, you will pass two poles that mark the course of a
natural gas pipeline from the North Sea.

Walk past the houses of **West Horton** and **East
Horton**, passing East Horton Farmhouse B&B (www.
farmhousebandb.co.uk) and turning L onto a road
sometimes known as the Devil's Causeway, which
follows the course of an old Roman road. Turn R onto an
unsealed road, with views of Greensheen Hill to the NE,
and passing an old World War 2 pillbox on your R before
descending to cross the **Hetton Burn**. Pillboxes are a
familiar sight along the Northumberland coast (there is
another on the edge of the small wood on the rise ahead
of you), this having been the expected site of a possible
land invasion of Britain by Hitler's Germany. Bear L then
R, ascending then crossing a sealed road.

Continue uphill, then turn L onto a footpath just after
a plantation, where the road veers R. Walk alongside the

*Fields beside the
Devil's Causeway,
a Roman road
near East Horton*

plantation before turning R through a stile, then L above gorse and alongside the edge of the field. Pass the corner of the large wood, keeping along the edge of the field, then turn R onto a track that ascends towards the woods ahead, with the sandstone crags of Cockenheugh visible through a gap in the trees. On meeting the wood, turn L, until you reach the clear path on your R leading up to **St Cuthbert's Cave**.

> **St Cuthbert's Cave** is a beautiful sandstone overhang forming a natural shelter. According to popular belief, monks from Lindisfarne, forced to leave the island in the face of repeated Viking raids, rested here with the body of St Cuthbert and other precious relics in AD875.

Return to the main track and continue to the edge of the woods, then turn R and ascend to the top of the rise, on the shoulder of **Greensheen Hill**. Ahead across the fields is the course of St Oswald's Way, passing just below Fawcett Hill, with Virgin Hill Woods to the R of this.

> **Holburn Lake and Moss**, just on the other side of Greensheen Hill, is an important area for birdlife, including migrant species such as greylag and pink-footed geese, and is a SPA and a RAMSAR site.

St Cuthbert's Cave, where monks fleeing from Lindisfarne Priory are said to have sheltered with the remains of St Cuthbert

Descend across the fields then ascend again to meet SOW and the NCP coming in from the R. Here you get your first breathtaking view of the coast around Holy Island – one which can be enhanced by hiking up to the high ground just off the route on your R.

From the stile at the junction of the trails, turn L onto a track, with views of Holy Island on your R, to arrive at **Shiellow Wood**. After entering the wood, take the signposted track on your R, pass another track and then Shiellow Crag House, both on your R. Keep straight ahead, crossing a stream by way of a small bridge, then cross a track, keeping straight ahead on a path signposted to Fenwick. Cross a series of small wooden bridges and streams, with clear waymarkings, to reach a stile at the edge of the wood. Continue alongside fields, following the course of what was once an old lane known as Dolly Gibson's Lonnen.

Map continues on page 76

The woods on your left, **Kyloe Woods**, are an important reserve for the red squirrel, and it was here that some of the first *leylandii cypress* stock – now a popular hybrid hedging shrub – was grown in the 19th century.

Veer L to arrive at a farm, before turning R and following the road (once part of the Great North Road) downhill to the small settlement of **Fenwick**.

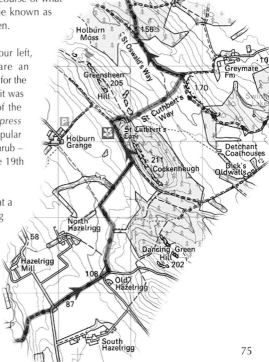

There is no longer any accommodation in Fenwick, so walkers will need to continue to West Mains (or Beal). Turn L along the B6353 (towards West Kyloe), then R onto a minor road that leads past Mount Hooly and joins the A1 just a short distance from the Lindisfarne Inn (www. inncollectiongroup.com/lindisfarne-inn, tel 01289 01289 751923) at **West Mains** (25min from Fenwick). To continue to Beal, follow the road towards Holy Island from West Mains (allow 15min).

The X15 and X18 buses stop outside the Lindisfarne Inn, West Mains.

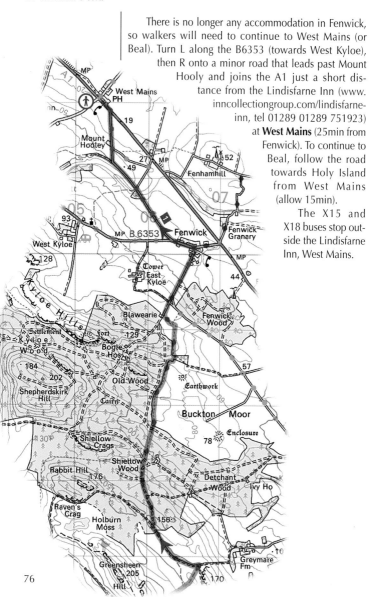

STAGE 5

West Mains to Holy Island

Start	Lindisfarne Inn, West Mains
Finish	Lindisfarne Priory, Holy Island
Distance	7½ miles (12km)
Time	2hr 45min (timing includes 1hr to cross the sands)
Maps	OS Explorer 340; OS Landranger 75
Access	X15 and X18 buses from Berwick-upon-Tweed/ Newcastle to West Mains
Accommodation	Either a second night at the Lindisfarne Inn in West Mains if visiting Holy Island as a day trip; or the Crown & Anchor or several other options on Holy Island itself.
Note	For the final part of the route across the sands to Holy Island you must observe the safe crossing times, see https://holyislandcrossingtimes.northumberland.gov.uk

A short and very easy stage, this follows the 'Pilgrim's Way' across the sands to Holy Island. From West Mains, retrace your steps to Fenwick to rejoin the official SCW route. Alternatively, a more direct option is to simply head down the road past Beal – there is a cycle track beside the road which is pleasant enough – to rejoin the main route at the causeway.

Even if you do not plan to stay on Holy Island and intend to visit as a 'day trip' (for example, between two nights at West Mains), you must still time your return to coincide with safe crossing times.

Continue through **Fenwick** on the B6353, cross the A1 and continue on the road straight ahead, past **Fenwick Granary**. Veer R past the farm, crossing a cattle grid, then turn L onto a path and ascend, passing a disused quarry. Turn R onto a road to reach a track on your L known as Fishers Back Road, which leads in a little under 1½ miles (2km) to the crossing point for the East Coast Main Line.

In 2022, National Rail closed the crossing here – in theory temporarily, although the closure may become permanent. Assuming the closure is permanent, continue

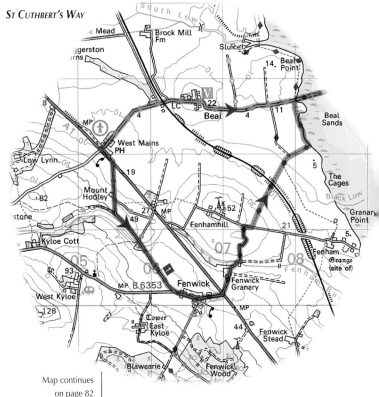

Map continues
on page 82

along the road past Fishers Back Road, towards Fenham, and cross the **railway line** by the road bridge. Just after the bridge a track on your L leads back alongside the railway line to rejoin SCW (adding around ¾ of a mile/1.1km to the original route). Alternatively, you could continue into Fenham, turn L towards Granary Point, then follow a path L past the marshland of The Cages and Black Low to rejoin the original route of SCW at a footbridge over Beal Cast (this adds about 1 mile/1.6km to the original route). If the foot crossing reopens: go down Fishers Back Road to the East Coast **Main Line**, where it is essential that you call the signal box before crossing, using the phone provided, to check whether there are any trains

Following the Pilgrim's Route across the sands to Holy Island

approaching. **Do not** cross the railway lines before you have been given the all clear. Then go straight ahead and cross the footbridge over Beal Cast.

From the footbridge over Beal Cast, head down through the (temporary) caravan site, and follow the track straight ahead, before turning R onto a path and then L along the coast to the **Holy Island causeway**. ▶

After confirming the safe crossing times at the entrance to the Holy Island causeway, follow the road for a short distance, crossing the bridge over South Low to the first refuge box. It takes at least 1hr for the 2½-mile (4.5km) crossing over the sands – some even advise allowing up to 2hr if the sand is soft – and you can only cross them safely during the middle of the safe crossing period. Ideally, you should aim to *complete* your crossing by the midpoint of the safe crossing period.

The OS maps have the route of SCW marked along the causeway, but instead strike out ESE across the sands along the Pilgrim's Route, following the clear line of the marker poles. Water generally lies in patches across the sands even at low tide, so crossing barefoot may be preferable, or in sandals or wellies. Note the refuge box atop one of the marker poles – people do still get stranded crossing to Holy Island, both on the sands and

Beal, just 1 mile (1.5km) up the road to the W, takes its name from 'bee hill', and is thought to have supplied honey to Holy Island.

HOLY ISLAND

The Irish monk St Aidan founded a **priory** on Holy Island (Lindisfarne) in AD635, at the request of the Anglo-Saxon King Oswald. Holy Island was to become one of the most important early centres of Christianity in England, responsible for producing the beautiful Lindisfarne Gospels in the early 700s. Nothing remains of the first monastery, which was destroyed by Viking raids in the late eighth and ninth centuries, with the monks themselves departing in 875. In 1083 the monastery was refounded by the Bishop of Durham, and the rather magnificent red sandstone ruin seen today dates from between this time and the first half of the 12th century, with the monastic buildings added in the 13th century and later.

Directly opposite the entrance to the priory is **St Mary's Church**, the oldest church on Holy Island. Much of the building dates from the 13th century, but some elements of an earlier building are still visible – including some Saxon details. The church was restored in the 19th century, and has stained glass by Franz Mayer.

Just to the south of the priory is a small knoll known as the Heugh, where there was once a small fort. The memorial cross is by Edwin Lutyens,   the architect responsible for renovating Lindisfarne Castle in the early 1900s. The

The 'rainbow arch' at the ruins of Lindisfarne Priory. This rib from the priory's vault survived the collapse of the surrounding roof and tower above it

Heugh is part of the Holy Island Dyke, an outcrop of the Whin Sill, upon which the castle is also built. The views are excellent – note the navigation posts on Ross Sands, over on the mainland. A short distance offshore, to the west of the priory and the Heugh, is a

Lindisfarne Castle

small island, where St Cuthbert once had a monastic cell, and the remains of a medieval chapel can still be seen. Elsewhere in the village you will find the Lindisfarne Centre (www.lindisfarnecentre.org), with exhibitions and a shop, the St Cuthbert Centre (www.holyisland-stcuthbert.org), and St Aiden's Winery (www.lindisfarnemead.com), home of the well-known local mead. The village cross in the market square dates from 1828.

The ancient sand dune systems of Holy Island are rich in flowers and grasses, supporting species such as coral-root orchid and the endemic Lindisfarne helleborine.

West of the castle at Castle Point is a well-preserved group of limekilns (for a good appreciation of how they would have looked when working, see the large oil painting by John Moore from 1877 in the entrance hall of the castle, which depicts the castle and priory with the limekilns burning in the moonlight). Above the east shore of Holy Island, just beyond the castle and the limekilns, you will often find carefully arranged cairns and piles of stones, and sometimes more elaborate creations – on one visit I saw a beautifully observed horse in small black and white stones – left by visitors and pilgrims. Beyond, the grey expanse of the North Sea stretches to the horizon. Just to the north of the castle is the small walled garden designed and laid out by Gertrude Jekyll in 1911, for Edward Hudson.

Accommodation on Holy Island includes the Crown & Anchor (www.holyislandcrown.co.uk, tel 01289 389215), the Lindisfarne Hotel (https://visitlindisfarne.com/listings/short-stays/lindisfarne-hotel, tel 01289 389273) and The Ship Inn (www.theshipinn-holyisland.co.uk, tel 01289 389311).

the causeway, although there is no reason to do so, providing you observe the safe crossing times. As you walk, keep an eye out for waterfowl, of which these vast tidal flats have plenty. You might also reflect on how this beautiful tidal area was used for bombing practice during World War 2.

Approximately 1hr after leaving the road by South Low, you arrive at **Chare Ends** on Holy Island (Lindisfarne). Follow the road straight ahead and around to the R, passing the substantial car park and striding into the small village of **Holy Island**.

Although Holy Island marks one end of St Cuthbert's Way, it really is well worth continuing up the coast to Berwick-upon-Tweed, following a section of the Northumberland Coast Path – it's some of the loveliest coastal scenery in Britain, and there are good rail connections from Berwick as well as bus routes back down the coast towards Newcastle.

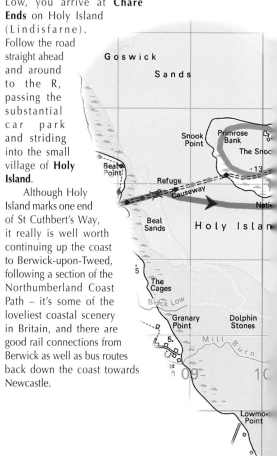

Walks around Holy Island

There are several short walks that allow you to explore Holy Island further. The first, and most obvious, is to continue E from the priory then N from **Lindisfarne Castle**, following the coast and completing a circuit of the island (3 miles (5km), allow 1½hr). As you walk around the harbour (known as the Ouse) from the priory to reach the castle, note the upturned fishing boats, the hulls of which have been sawn in half and converted into small sheds.

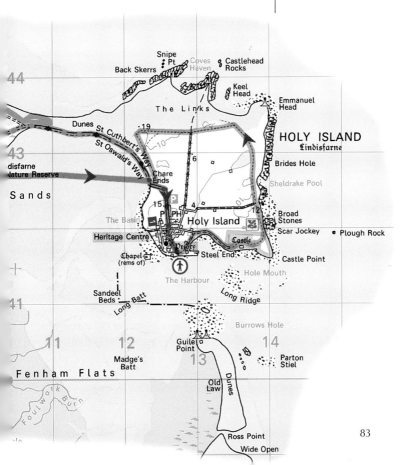

Lindisfarne Castle, which was built in 1549–50, was bought by Edward Hudson (founder of *Country Life* magazine) in 1901, and transformed into a home by architect Edwin Lutyens. It occupies a spectacular position on a steep outcrop of the Whin Sill, and its interior is a fascinating warren of passages and vaulted rooms. The castle provided a suitably atmospheric setting for Roman Polanski's 1966 film *Cul-de-Sac*.

On the eastern side of the island you pass the Lough, a shallow freshwater lake (perhaps established by the monks as a fresh water supply or for fish) where there is a hide. Much of the trail here follows an old wagon route used for transporting lime from the kilns at Castle Point. After turning west before the navigation post at **Emmanuel Head**, you pass a trail on the right which can be followed to Nessend on the northern shore of the island. The dune grassland here is a good place to see bloody cranesbill and other flowers. Iron was worked at **Coves Haven**, just west of here, during the 18th century, and exported to Falkirk. Beyond Coves Haven the limestone outcrop of **Back Skerrs** projects out into the sea. Return to the main route, then turn S, passing old limekilns and return to the car park.

Another option is to follow a shorter circuit around **The Snook** – an old dune system and once the focus of coal mining activity – starting and finishing at a parking area part way back along the road to the causeway (2 miles/3.5km, allow 1hr). Alternatively, from the same start/finish point, you can explore The Big Bank (1½ miles/2.5km, allow 45min). Note that the section of the causeway leading from Holy Island to The Snook is also covered by water at high tide, so either of these excursions needs to be timed to fit within safe crossing times.

STAGE 6

Holy Island to Berwick-upon-Tweed

Start	Lindisfarne Priory, Holy Island
Finish	Quayside, Berwick-upon-Tweed
Distance	11½ miles (18.5km)
Time	5hr 30min (including 1hr to cross the sands)
Maps	OS Explorer 340, 341 and 346; OS Landranger 75
Access	The X15 and X18 Berwick-upon-Tweed–Newcastle bus and the 477 Berwick-upon-Tweed–Holy Island stop at Beal/Holy Island road end. From the finish at Berwick-upon-Tweed there are regular and frequent rail services to many destinations, including London, Edinburgh and Newcastle
Accommodation	There is plenty of choice of accommodation in Berwick-upon-Tweed, including The King's Head and Berwick YHA
Note	There is a possible danger of **unexploded ordnance** around Goswick Sands and the dunes behind Cheswick Sands. Pay attention to warning signs

This is an easy day with some road walking – much of which can be avoided by following the coast itself, including Goswick and Cheswick Sands – and some of the finest coastal scenery anywhere in the UK. If you have stayed at West Mains instead of on Holy Island, follow the road down to the causeway (2 miles or 3km), and pick up the route there.

From **Holy Island**, follow the Pilgrim's Route across the sands at low tide (allow at least 1hr). From the car park just inland from the causeway, follow the NCP sign and head N along the coast, passing initially between a double row of concrete anti-tank blocks from World War 2, and then passing a pair of World War 2 pillboxes on your left. The path here is apt to be marshy and the tide can reach quite high, in which case there are sections of path higher up on the bank on the left if necessary.

After reaching a perpendicular track, turn R onto this and cross above the **sluice gates** over South Low. The path bends round to the R then L again, heading for the buildings of **Beachcomber House** and the ruins of a World War 2 observation tower.

> **Goswick Sands** was used for live bombing practice during World War 2 (hence the observation tower), and there is still a possible danger of unexploded ordnance in this area. Signs warn visitors not to touch or pick up any metal objects.

The route on from Beachcomber House follows several sections of road or the National Cycle Network 1 track, much of which can be avoided by walking along parts of the beach, crossing Goswick Sands and Cheswick Sands, and later Cocklawburn Beach. This will be partly dependent on the tides, especially at the north end of Cheswick Sands, around the rocks of Far Skerr – and read the signs warning of the potential danger of live ordnance on Goswick Sands. Check the Lindisfarne safe crossing times for an indication of the tides here. In any

Map continues
on page 89

Snipe Pt
Back Skerrs
Coves Haven
Castlehead Rocks
Keel Head
Emmanuel Head
The Links
Dunes
St Cuthbert's Way
St Oswald's Way
19
10
6
HOLY ISLAND
Lindisfarne
Brides Hole
Sheldrake Pool
Chare Ends
15
P
4
12
Broad Stones
The Basin
P PH
Holy Island
Scar Jockey
Heritage Centre
Priory
Castle
Chapel (rems of)
Steel End
Castle Point
The Harbour
Hole Mouth
Sandeel Beds
Long Batt
Long Ridge
Guile Point

Cheswick Sands, site of some of the tallest sand dunes on the Northumberland coast, looking S to Goswick Sands

87

Map continues
on page 91

case, there are several points at which you can cross from the beach to the road or track, as marked on the map. Walking times will be similar either way.

From the former campsite, continue straight ahead on the road, passing yet another golf course on your right (this is the last one), and turning L on the road after the **clubhouse**.

Do not cross the East Coast Main Line. Instead take the path on your R just before the railway crossing, alongside the golf practice range, then R at the end of this, and L onto an embankment alongside the N end of the golf course.

Around 4 miles (6.5km) from the Holy Island causeway you reach a road end and National Cycle Network 1. Whether or not you intend to follow the beach, take the path to the R here, which leads up onto the dunes and down onto the broad sweep of **Cheswick Sands**, for a view of what is surely one of the most beautiful stretches of coastline anywhere in the UK. The dunes here are some of the highest of the Northumberland coast. (Caution: the fenced area behind and inland from the dunes was once an old military firing range, and signs warn not to walk in this area due to the danger of unexploded ordnance.)

To follow the road rather than the beach, retrace your steps and go along the cycle route, passing a pond on your L (a former limestone quarry), and footpaths down to the beach and **Cocklawburn Dunes Nature Reserve** and Middle and Far Skerrs on your R.

> **The Skerrs** here are exposed sections of folded limestone projecting into the sea, and are particularly rich in fossils. You will also find the ruins of an old limekiln near Middle Skerr, a further reminder of the former importance of this industry in the area (as well as limestone, sandstone was also quarried locally, and there was an important coal mine just inland from here at Scremerston).

Pass a prominent World War 2 gun turret on your R, followed by a small car park and a path down

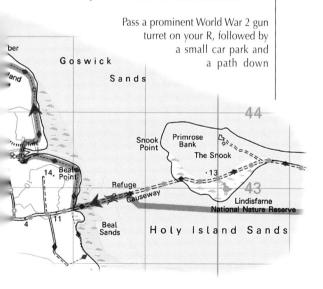

to **Cocklawburn Beach**. Saltpan Rocks just to the N of here was once the site of a small salt-making industry, where seawater was evaporated in large pans heated by coal. Continue past **Sea House** before following a clifftop path along the narrow strip of land between the cliffs and the railway line, above the pink sandstone cliffs of **Hud's Head**. Turn R and follow the path down to the promenade at **Spittal** on the edge of **Berwick-upon-Tweed**.

Follow the promenade to its end, noting the information boards on the English painter LS Lowry, who visited Berwick-upon-Tweed many times from the mid-1930s until his death in 1976. Pass an old chimney on your L and go around the point to a car park, then L onto a road and R onto Dock Road and Main Street. Follow this to the Old Bridge, completed in 1626, with views of the impressive Elizabethan walls on the other side of the Tweed. Cross the bridge (note the sundial on the R at the far end), and turn R to reach an anchor sculpture on the cobbled quayside, which now marks the end of the

The Old Bridge in Berwick-upon-Tweed, built in 1611

90

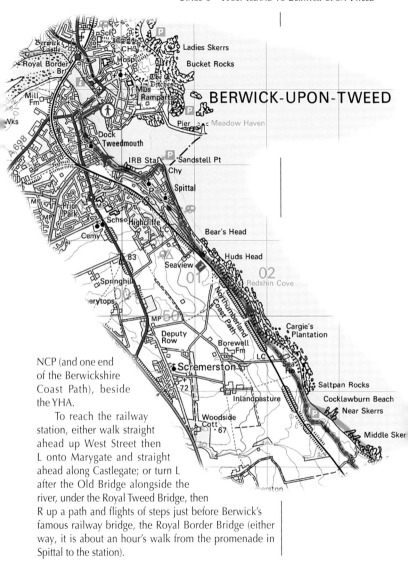

NCP (and one end of the Berwickshire Coast Path), beside the YHA.

To reach the railway station, either walk straight ahead up West Street then L onto Marygate and straight ahead along Castlegate; or turn L after the Old Bridge alongside the river, under the Royal Tweed Bridge, then R up a path and flights of steps just before Berwick's famous railway bridge, the Royal Border Bridge (either way, it is about an hour's walk from the promenade in Spittal to the station).

BERWICK-UPON-TWEED

Berwick-upon-Tweed, with its trio of bridges spanning the River Tweed, has an old town centre encircled by one of the most complete sections of Elizabethan fortifications anywhere in Britain. Passed repeatedly back and forth between English and Scottish hands – it has been English since 1482 – Berwick was sacked more than a dozen times between the 11th and 15th centuries. The medieval walls were begun by Edward I in 1296. However, these were not sufficient protection against artillery and in 1558 an elaborate, Italianate system of bastions was designed by Richard Lee (previously responsible for the defences at Portsmouth). The Old Bridge was completed in 1626. The Royal Border Bridge, 1847–50, soars across the Tweed like a Roman aqueduct, its 28 arches carrying the East Coast Main Line into Berwick station at a height of 38.5m. Between the two is the concrete Royal Tweed Bridge, built in the 1920s.

The Church of the Holy Trinity was built in the 1650s, with some restoration in the 19th century. In the south aisle is a monument to Colonel Fenwicke, who commissioned the church. The windows include 16th–17th-century Dutch and Flemish stained glass. Berwick Castle – which stood at one corner of the older, medieval walls – was demolished in the 19th century to make way for the railway station, which stands on the site of the Great Hall. There is a Lowry Trail (www.visitberwick.com), which visits many of the places in Berwick painted by LS Lowry.

Accommodation in Berwick-upon-Tweed includes YHA Berwick (www.yha.org.uk/hostel/yha-berwick, tel 0345 371 9676), The Queen's Head (www.grhotels.co.uk/queens-head-berwick, tel 01289 307852), The King's Head (www.kingsheadberwick.co.uk, tel 01289 331491) and The Cowrie Guesthouse (www.cowrieguesthouseberwick.co.uk, tel 01289 763781).

APPENDIX A

Route summary table

St Cuthbert's Way

Stage	Start	Finish	Distance	Time	Maps	Page
1	Melrose	Jedburgh	19½ miles (32km)	8hr 15min	OS Explorer 338 and OL16; OS Landranger 73	40
2	Jedburgh	Kirk Yetholm	16 miles (26km)	7hr 45min	OS Explorer OL16; OS Landranger 74	53
3	Kirk Yetholm	Wooler	13 miles (21km)	6hr 40min	OS Explorer OL16; OS Landranger 74 and 75	61
4	Wooler	West Mains	13 miles (21.5km)	5hr 25min	OS Explorer 340; OS Landranger 75	70
5	West Mains	Holy Island	7½ miles (12km)	2hr 45min	OS Explorer 340; OS Landranger 75	77
6	Holy Island	Berwick-upon-Tweed	11½ miles (18.5km)	5hr 30min	OS Explorer 340 and 341; OS Landranger 75	85

APPENDIX B
Glossary and pronunciation

bell	hill
brig	bridge
burn	stream
cleugh	ravine
coble	traditional open-top Northumberland fishing boat
flother	area of marsh or bog
harr	mist in coastal areas
haugh	low, level pasture or marshy area
heugh	crag, cliff or steep-sided hill
kirk	church
knowe	(pronounced 'now') low hill
law	hill
linn	waterfall
lonnen	lane
lough	(pronounced 'luff') shallow freshwater lake
moss	marshy or boggy area
pele	fortified tower
rigg	ridge
sike	stream
skerr (plural *skerries*)	rock outcropping into the sea, small rocky reef
snook	headland or point
stane	stone
steading	small farm settlement

APPENDIX C
Accommodation

Melrose
The George & Abbotsford Hotel
High Street,
Melrose
TD6 9PD
tel 01896 822308
www.georgeandabbotsford
melrose.co.uk

Fiorlin B&B
Abbey Street,
Melrose
TD6 9PX
tel 01896 822984
https://melrosebedandbreakfast.co.uk

The Station Hotel
26 Market Square,
Melrose
TD6 9BT
tel 01896 823147
https://stationhotelmelrose.com

Dryburgh
Dryburgh Abbey Hotel
Dryburgh,
St Boswells
TD6 0RQ
tel 01835 822261
www.dryburgh.co.uk

St Boswells
Buccleuch Arms Hotel
The Green,
St Boswells
TD6 0EW
tel 01835 822243
www.buccleucharms.com

Dryburgh Arms
Melbourne Place,
Newtown,
St Boswells
TD6 0PA
tel 01835 822704
https://dryburgharms.co.uk

Ancrum
Ale Water Cottage
Ancrum
https://alewatercottage.co.uk

Jedburgh
Meadhon House B&B
48 Castlegate,
Jedburgh
TD8 6BB
tel 01835 862504
www.meadhon.co.uk

Royal Hotel
21–23 Canongate,
Jedburgh
TD8 6AN
tel 01835 863152
www.royalhoteljedburgh.com

Morebattle
Templehall Hotel
Main Street,
Morebattle
TD5 8QQ
tel 01573 440249
www.templehallhotel.com

Kirk Yetholm

The Farmhouse at Yetholm Mill
Kirk Yetholm
tel 01573 420505
www.thefarmhouseatkirkyetholm.com

The Border Hotel
The Green,
Kirk Yetholm
TD5 8PQ
tel 01573 420237
www.borderhotel.co.uk

Mill House B&B
Main Street,
Kirk Yetholm
TD5 8PE
tel 01573 420604
https://millhouseyetholm.co.uk

The Plough Hotel
Main Street,
Town Yetholm
TD5 8RS
tel 01573 420215
www.theploughhotelyetholm.co.uk

Friends of Nature House Hostel
Waukford,
TD5 8PG
tel 01573 420639
https://friendsofnature.org.uk/houses/
kirk-yetholm

Hethpool

Mounthooly Bunkhouse (6km off route)
College Valley
tel 01668 216210
www.college-valley.co.uk/
accommodation/bunk-house

Wooler

The Tankerville Arms Hotel
Wooler
NE71 6AD
tel 01668 281581
www.tankervillehotel.co.uk

Tilldale House B&B
34/40 High Street,
Wooler
NE71 6BG
tel 01668 281450
www.tilldalehouse.co.uk

Wooler YHA
30 Cheviot St,
Wooler
NE71 6LW
tel 0345 260 2931
www.yha.org.uk/hostel/yha-wooler

East Horton

East Horton Farmhouse B&B
East Horton
NE71 6EZ
tel 01668 215216
www.farmhousebandb.co.uk

West Mains/Beal

Lindisfarne Inn
West Mains,
Beal
TD15 2PD
tel 01289 751923
www.inncollectiongroup.com/
lindisfarne-inn

Holy Island

The Crown & Anchor
The Market Place,
Holy Island
TD15 2RX
tel 01289 389215
www.holyislandcrown.co.uk

The Lindisfarne Hotel
Holy Island
TD15 2SQ
tel 01289 389273
https://visitlindisfarne.com/listings/
short-stays/lindisfarne-hotel

The Ship Inn
Marygate,
Holy Island
TD15 2SJ
tel 01289 389311
www.theshipinn-holyisland.co.uk

For more accommodation on Holy
Island see www.lindisfarne.org.uk

Berwick-upon-Tweed

The Walls B&B
8 Quay Walls,
Berwick-upon-Tweed
TD15 1HB
tel 01289 330233
www.thewallsberwick.com

Berwick-upon-Tweed YHA
Dewars Lane Granary,
Dewars Lane,
Berwick-upon-Tweed
TD15 1HJ
tel 0845 371 9676
www.yha.org.uk/hostel/berwick

The Queen's Head
6 Sandgate,
Berwick-upon-Tweed
TD15 1EP
tel 01289 307852
www.grhotels.co.uk/
queens-head-berwick

The King's Head
56 Church Street,
Berwick-upon-Tweed
TD15 1DX
tel 01289 331491
www.kingsheadberwick.co.uk

The Cowrie Guesthouse
8 Quay Walls,
Berwick-upon-Tweed
TD15 1HB
tel 01289 763781
www.cowrieguesthouseberwick.co.uk

APPENDIX D
Useful contacts

Tourist information
Visit Northumberland
www.visitnorthumberland.com

Visit Northeast England
www.visitnortheastengland.com

Northumberland Coast
www.northumberlandcoastpath.org
www.northumberlandcoastaonb.org

Northumberland National Park
www.northumberlandnationalpark.org.uk

Northumberland Wildlife Trust
www.nwt.org.uk

Hadrian's Wall Country
www.hadrians-wall.org

Lindisfarne
www.lindisfarne.org.uk

Visit Scotland
www.visitscotland.com

Undiscovered Scotland
www.undiscoveredscotland.co.uk

Local tourist information offices

Borders
Jedburgh tel 01835 863170
Melrose tel 01896 822283

Northumberland
Berwick-upon-Tweed tel 01670 622155
Wooler tel 01668 282123

Walks – online resources
North Sea Trail
www.northseatrail.org

St Cuthbert's Way
www.stcuthbertsway.info

Northumberland National Park
www.northumberlandnationalpark.org.uk

Northumberland Coast
www.northumberlandcoastpath.org
www.northumberlandcoastaonb.org

Cheviot Walks
www.cheviotwalks.co.uk

Safe crossing times for Holy Island
Northumberland County Council
https://holyislandcrossingtimes.
northumberland.gov.uk

Wildlife and heritage tours
Northern Experience Wildlife Tours
tel 01670 827465
www.northernexperiencewildlifetours.
co.uk

**Guided/self-guided walking holidays
and luggage services**
Shepherds Walks
www.shepherdswalks.co.uk

Sherpa Van
www.sherpavan.com

Carry Lite
www.carrylite.co.uk

Transport operators
London North Eastern Railway
www.lner.co.uk

National Rail Enquiries
www.nationalrail.co.uk

Arriva
www.arrivabus.co.uk

Glen Valley Tours
tel 01668 281578
www.glenvalley.co.uk

Go North East
www.gonortheast.co.uk/services

Border's Buses
tel 01289 308719
www.bordersbuses.co.uk

Maps and guidebooks
The Map Shop
www.themapshop.co.uk

Ordnance Survey
www.ordnancesurvey.co.uk

Natural History Bookshop
www.nhbs.com

Stanfords
www.stanfords.co.uk

Other
Ad Gefrin
(archaeology of the Cheviot Hills)
www.gefrin.com

Disused Stations (disused railway lines
and stations)
www.disused-stations.org.uk

National Trails
www.nationaltrail.co.uk

Scottish Gypsies
www.scottishgypsies.co.uk

Sites of Special Scientific Interest
(England)
www.sssi.naturalengland.org.uk

Scottish Natural Heritage
www.nature.scot

Trinity House (lighthouses)
www.trinityhouse.co.uk

Walter Scott Digital Archive
www.walterscott.lib.ed.ac.uk

APPENDIX E
Further reading

Guidebooks

Ron Shaw, *St Cuthbert's Way: The Official Guide* (2nd edition; Birlinn, 2011)

Iain Robson, *Northumberland Coast Path* (Northumberland County Council, 2015)

Tony Hopkins, *Northumberland: The Official National Park Guide* (David & Charles, 2002)

Mary Low, *St Cuthbert's Way: A Pilgrim's Companion* (Wild Goose Publications, 2000)

History, art and architecture

Bede, *The Age of Bede* (Penguin, 2004)

Bede, *The Ecclesiastical History of the English Church and People* (Penguin, 1991)

Stan Beckensall, *Northumberland's Hidden History* (Amberley, 2009)

Stan Beckensall, *Prehistoric Rock Art of Northumberland* (The History Press, 2001)

Stan Beckensall, *Northumberland: Shadows of the Past* (NPI Media, 2005)

PH Blair, *Northumbria in the Days of Bede* (Victor Gollancz, 1976)

William Brockie, *The Gypsies of Yetholm* (Rutherford, 1884)

Michelle P Brown, *The Lindisfarne Gospels and the Early Medieval Period* (British Library, 2010)

Michelle P Brown, *The Lindisfarne Gospels: Society, Spirituality and the Scribe* (British Library, 2003)

Michelle P Brown, *Painted Labyrinth: The World of the Lindisfarne Gospels* (British Library, 2003)

Tom Cadwallender (ed.), *Exploring the Historic Buildings of the Northumberland Coast Area of Outstanding Natural Beauty* (Northumberland County Council, 2006)

J Campbell, *The Anglo-Saxons* (Penguin, 1991)

Keith Durham, *Strongholds of the Border: Fortifications of the Anglo-Scottish Border 1296–1603* (Osprey, 2008)

DH Farmer, *The Oxford Dictionary of Saints* (Oxford, 2003)

Richard Fawcett, *Scottish Abbeys and Priories* (Historic Scotland, 1993)

Paul Frodsham, *Archaeology in Northumberland National Park* (Council for British Archaeology, 2004)

PA Graham, *Highways and Byeways in Northumbria* (Macmillan, 1920)

Kitty Kruft, John Dunbar and Richard Fawcett, *The Buildings of Scotland: The Borders* (Yale, 2006)

Nikolaus Pevsner and Ian Richmond, *The Buildings of England: Northumberland* (Yale, 2002)

Eric Robson, *The Border Line: The Story of the England–Scotland Border* (Frances Lincoln, 2007)

David Rollason, *Northumbria, 500–1100: Creation and Destruction of a Kingdom* (Cambridge, 2007)

FM Stenton, *Anglo-Saxon England* (Oxford, 1946)

AV Tokely, *The Kirk Yetholm Gypsies* (Hawick Archaeological Society, 2004)

Margaret Tynedale, *Legends and Folklore of Northumbria* (Collins, 1930)

Wildlife and plants

Marjorie Blamey and Richard Fitter, *Wild Flowers of Britain and Ireland* (A & C Black, 2003)

Tom Cadwallender (ed.), *Bird Watching on the Northumberland Coast Area of Outstanding Natural Beauty and Heritage Coast* (Northumberland County Council, 2007)

Tom Cadwallender (ed.), *Exploring the Plantlife of the Northumberland Coast Area of Outstanding Natural Beauty* (Northumberland County Council, 2006)

Wendy Dickson, *The Wildflowers of Coastal Northumberland: A Photographic Guide* (Keepdate, 2000)

Simon Harrap and David Nurney, *RSPB Pocket Guide to British Birds* (A & C Black, 2007)

Ian Kerr, *The Birds of Holy Island* (2nd edition; Ian Kerr, 2007)

Jane Lancaster, *Exploring the Shore in Northumberland and Berwickshire* (Northumberland County Council, 2004)

Jane Lancaster, *The Underwater World of Northumberland and Berwickshire* (Northumberland County Council, 2006)

Paul Sterry, *Collins Complete Guide to British Birds* (Collins, 2008)

GA Swan, *Flora of Northumberland* (Natural History Society of Northumbria, 1993)

Geology

Clive Crossley and Tom Cadwallender, *Explore the Geology and Landscape of the Northumberland Coast AONB* (Northumberland County Council, 2007)

P Stone, D Millward and B Young, *Northern England* (Regional Geology Guides) (British Geological Survey, 2010)

Literature

AJ Cronin, *The Stars Look Down* (Victor Gollancz, 1935)

Kevin Crossley-Holland (ed.), *The Anglo-Saxon World: An Anthology* (Oxford, 2009)

Rowena Farre, *A Time from the World* (Hutchinson, 1962)

Richard Hamer (ed.), *A Choice of Anglo-Saxon Verse* (Faber, 2006)

Kathleen Raine, *Farewell Happy Fields* (Hamish Hamilton, 1973)

Robert Westall, *The Machine Gunners* (Penguin, 1975)

LISTING OF UK CICERONE GUIDES

BRITISH ISLES CHALLENGES, COLLECTIONS AND ACTIVITIES

Cycling Land's End to John o' Groats
GreatWalks on the England Coast Path
The Big Rounds
The Book of the Bivvy
The Book of the Bothy
The Mountains of England & Wales:
  Vol 1 Wales
  Vol 2 England
The National Trails
Walking the End to End Trail

SHORT WALKS SERIES

Short Walks Hadrian's Wall
Short Walks in Arnside and Silverdale
Short Walks in Dumfries and Galloway
Short Walks in Nidderdale
Short Walks in the Lake District: Windermere Ambleside and Grasmere
Short Walks on the Malvern Hills
Short Walks in the Surrey Hills
Short Walks Winchester

SCOTLAND

Ben Nevis and Glen Coe
Cycle Touring in Northern Scotland
Cycling in the Hebrides
Great Mountain Days in Scotland
Mountain Biking in Southern and Central Scotland
Mountain Biking in West and North West Scotland
Not the West Highland Way Scotland
Scotland's Best Small Mountains
Scotland's Mountain Ridges
Scottish Wild Country Backpacking
Skye's Cuillin Ridge Traverse
The Borders Abbeys Way
The Great Glen Way
The Great Glen Way Map Booklet
The Hebridean Way
The Hebrides
The Isle of Mull

The Isle of Skye
The Skye Trail
The Southern Upland Way
The West Highland Way
The West Highland Way Map Booklet
Walking Ben Lawers, Rannoch and Atholl
Walking in the Cairngorms
Walking in the Pentland Hills
Walking in the Scottish Borders
Walking in the Southern Uplands
Walking in Torridon, Fisherfield, Fannichs and An Teallach
Walking Loch Lomond and the Trossachs
Walking on Arran
Walking on Harris and Lewis
Walking on Jura, Islay and Colonsay
Walking on Rum and the Small Isles
Walking on the Orkney and Shetland Isles
Walking on Uist and Barra
Walking the Cape Wrath Trail
Walking the Corbetts
  Vol 1 South of the Great Glen
  Vol 2 North of the Great Glen
Walking the Galloway Hills
Walking the John o' Groats Trail
Walking the Munros
  Vol 1 – Southern, Central and Western Highlands
  Vol 2 – Northern Highlands and the Cairngorms
Winter Climbs: Ben Nevis and Glen Coe

NORTHERN ENGLAND ROUTES

Cycling the Reivers Route
Cycling the Way of the Roses
Hadrian's Cycleway
Hadrian's Wall Path
Hadrian's Wall Path Map Booklet
The Coast to Coast Cycle Route
The Coast to Coast Walk
The Coast to Coast Walk Map Booklet
The Pennine Way
The Pennine Way Map Booklet
Walking the Dales Way
Walking the Dales Way Map Booklet

NORTH-EAST ENGLAND, YORKSHIRE DALES AND PENNINES

Cycling in the Yorkshire Dales
Great Mountain Days in the Pennines
Mountain Biking in the Yorkshire Dales
The Cleveland Way and the Yorkshire Wolds Way
The Cleveland Way Map Booklet
The North York Moors
The Reivers Way
Trail and Fell Running in the Yorkshire Dales
Walking in County Durham
Walking in Northumberland
Walking in the North Pennines
Walking in the Yorkshire Dales: North and East
Walking in the Yorkshire Dales: South and West
Walking St Cuthbert's Way
Walking St Oswald's Way and Northumberland Coast Path

NORTH-WEST ENGLAND AND THE ISLE OF MAN

Cycling the Pennine Bridleway
Isle of Man Coastal Path
The Lancashire Cycleway
The Lune Valley and Howgills
Walking in Cumbria's Eden Valley
Walking in Lancashire
Walking in the Forest of Bowland and Pendle
Walking on the Isle of Man
Walking on the West Pennine Moors
Walking the Ribble Way
Walks in Silverdale and Arnside

LAKE DISTRICT

Bikepacking in the Lake District
Cycling in the Lake District
Great Mountain Days in the Lake District
Joss Naylor's Lakes, Meres and Waters of the Lake District
Lake District Winter Climbs
Lake District: High Level and Fell Walks
Lake District: Low Level and Lake Walks

ONE€

r next adventure,
d the world...

ackpacking,
g, ski touring,
worldwide.

ation.

For full information on all our
guides, books and eBooks,
visit our website:
www.cicerone.co.uk